So You Want to [illegible] Successful Coll[illegible]

Effective College Creation and Profitable Management:
A Complete Guide for The Principal, Stakeholders and Staff

David A Bryden
BA (Hons); Dip.Ed.Man.; Cert.Ed.;CELTA; MRICS

AuthorHouse™ UK Ltd.
500 Avebury Boulevard
Central Milton Keynes, MK9 2BE
www.authorhouse.co.uk
Phone: 08001974150

The author acknowledges the contribution of Professor John Howard MA, BA (Hons) CIM to the contents of the marketing chapter of this volume.

First published by AuthorHouse 4/8/2010

ISBN: 978-1-4490-8562-9 (sc)

This book is printed on acid-free paper.

Table of Contents

INTRODUCTION

"Education. Education. Education." Tony Blair-British Prime Minister (1997)

The purpose of this publication is to offer advice about how to set up and successfully run a college! There are hundreds of people and organisations who, for the best reasons, believe that renting a few rooms, buying desks, chairs and some books and hiring people to teach will contribute to education and make them rich. One or both of these may happen but experience shows that it is more likely that little learning will take place and the rewards will not lead to wealth but poverty, as the costs of rent, council tax, marketing and salaries exceed the income from those students who DO enrol and pay. There are always many more students whose initial enquiry is never turned into physical attendance. Some enter the country on student visas, never enrol, and disappear.

This guide is written from the combined expertise of a group of professionals whose experience and association in the business of providing learning covers half a century in more than 50 countries.

It shows how to legally recruit students who will pay and who want to learn; it describes effective learning environments; it shows how students themselves are the best and lowest-cost marketing tool; it shows ,in short,how to make money not lose it and how to provide successful and cost-effective learning to those who will benefit most.

We have divided the key points into separate chapters arranged as follows :

1] **Acquisition and Income**
2] **Design and Administration**
3] **Students**
4] **Courses**
5] **Awarding bodies and Academic Partners**
6] **Staff**
7] **Monitoring and Inspections**
8] **Marketing**

The intention is to guide the reader, perhaps a stakeholder, director, entrepreneur, philanthropist, business tycoon, or educational trust, through each of the stages from acquiring premises to planning for inspections. Even if you already provide educational services in your own college, there will be guidance here to make your enterprise more effective, the teaching more interesting and will make the courses those that more students will want to pursue.

For college **Principals**, this volume offers essential information about what is needed to guide a college through all stages of effectiveness and efficiency; it provides checklists of documentation and advice on management, teaching, assessment, human resource management and marketing. It equips Principals to become the figurehead of the organisation.

We have tried to avoid excessive '*eduspeak*' the language used by those professionals in the education industry although key words, phrases and acronyms are included in **Appendix 1**

As a caution, too many people have spent too much money - probably for all the right reasons - and tried to set up learning institutions without detailed and thorough preparation or with insufficient knowledge and experience. It is intended throughout to point out where caution is necessary, where professional advice should be sought and where money needs and does not need to be spent. In the end, all aspects described here are interlinked; simple economics demand that income exceeds expenditure, that teachers teach effectively, that qualifications are worth having and that marketing costs are proportional to reward.

If the above qualities are achieved, there is no reason why the college's aims, ambitions, mission statement and income cannot be as you would want. Read on and find out how.

Most colleges are owned by **stakeholders**, often directors, academics or shareholders of the academic / educational company or are managed by a local authority. The stakeholders may or may not be educational professionals. If they are, some of the roles described may be undertaken by some of the stakeholders themselves. If they are simply shareholders or directors, all of the roles identified in Chapter Six will consist of salaried staff or self-employed professionals.

One of the stakeholders should be a qualified accountant or if not, an independent firm of **accountants** should be engaged; their task is to work with the Bursar and when required produce the accounts showing the financial status of the college.

There are some caveats to explain first :

For the use of **He / him**, **his**, the female **She / her** are to be assumed to be of equal status.

The word '**teacher**' is used throughout to refer to anyone delivering a course, lecturing to students or assessing or mentoring their work. It includes lecturer, professor, trainer, tutor etc.

The word '**College**' applies to any building, suite of rooms or establishment where learning is to take place. It includes Institute, Institution, Academy, School etc.

TERMS AND SEMESTERS.

In Great Britain, the academic year begins on the first day of September. On this date, schoolchildren move up to the next level of education and those who have completed their studies leave school permanently or begin higher education at university or college. It is usually the beginning of the college year.

In Great Britain, the academic year in Further Education [FE] and Higher Education [HE] is usually divided into terms or semesters. A term implies a period of learning dictated by a finite end date; in Great Britain, the autumn term starts in September and ends in time for Christmas, a holiday period covering 25th December and 1st January, New year. The next or Spring term ends whenever the Easter holiday occurs but for religious reason the date of Easter can vary by several weeks. Therefore, sometimes the Spring term is short (8 weeks) and in other years, it can extend to 12 weeks or so.

To avoid this irregular learning pattern some colleges choose to operate either with 3 Semesters of regular and fixed length which can be of 10, 11 or 12 teaching weeks or colleges can elect to offer 2 semesters of about 18 teaching weeks. A total of 36 teaching weeks is usually considered the length of the academic year.

An Autumn semester would begin in September with Enrolment and Induction - when new students are introduced to each other, their teachers and their college - and the semester would run for (say) 11 weeks with a one-week holiday in early November, a 3-week holiday over Christmas and a restart in early January. There would then be one week of revision or the making up of missed classes followed by examinations.

A further 3-week holiday takes place before the spring term of 11 weeks begins at the end of February. Again, a holiday of 2 weeks occurs around Easter but in each semester, the number of teaching weeks and therefore the number of lessons is consistent.

After further revision and examinations in May, the summer semester begins and runs for 11 weeks followed again by revision week and examinations. After a short holiday, the new college year begins in again in September.

Definitions : in this book the following definitions are used throughout :

Curriculum : this is defined by *Stenhouse* (1976) as :

"...an attempt to communicate the essential principles and features of an education proposal in such a form that it is open to critical scrutiny and capable of effective translation into practice."

Throughout this book this definition, and those following, will be used :

the **Curriculum** : a list of all the separate courses to be successfully undertaken to complete the qualification / programme.

Syllabus : a brief description of the content of each separate course which makes up the overall curriculum.

Course programme : a detailed week-by-week timetable of the contents of the syllabus.

Lesson Plan : the content of each day's teaching of the course programme.

1] ACQUISITION and INCOME

"Location. Location. Location." Phil Spencer Property Developer (2009)

1.01 BUY OR RENT?

To acquire a building in which to run a college is both expensive and risky; **freehold** investments are subject to market forces and what was purchased for a fair price may, at a later date, be found to be worth less than its purchase price. There are of course advantages; repairs, alterations and improvements can be carried out and the value is absorbed into ownership whereas those improvements to rental property do not benefit you the **lessee** but the building's owner, the **lessor.**

If the property is bought on a loan or mortgage, then the cost of the yearly repayments including interest become an expense chargeable against profit and on which tax will not be payable. If the property is acquired with capital, an accountant will notionalise the loss of income from the capital NOT invested in the money market or another income-generating enterprise (the opportunity cost) and this too will feature in the balance sheet at the end of the year.

If the property is **leased** or **rented**, there is an easier exit from an unsuccessful business compared to owned property; at the expiry of the lease, there is no further obligation; should the business be successful, there is the opportunity to renew the lease for a further period of time at an agreed (and probably increased) rental sum. Often the improvements that have been carried our and paid for by the lessee have added to the value of the property and the rental will be increased because of it.

Whichever acquisition route is used, consideration should be given to the property's location and accommodation.

Whether leasing or purchasing, you will have to calculate how many students are essential to provide sufficient income to make the college viable as detailed in 1.05; therefore the chosen building will need to have been surveyed and plans produced so that the internal sub-divisions can be made to provide sufficient classrooms. Provision must also be made for space required by the administrative staff who are described in **Chapter Six**. The hygiene requirements for staff and students, the means of escape in case of fire and all other aspects of creating a college from its previous use, need to be approved by the relevant local authorities so it is advisable that a professional surveyor or architect be appointed to advise on, design, facilitate and obtain approvals for these changes.

1.02 LOCATION

It is unlikely that there are no other education establishments in the location you have chosen. If there are no others, then there is probably a good reason - the location is unsuitable. Therefore the college you are to establish must have individual qualities that differentiate it from all others; it must have a **unique selling point** (USP) Perhaps your college is the only one in the area which offers a particular set of courses;

perhaps the entry qualifications are less strict; perhaps fees are cheaper; perhaps it is easier to find; perhaps is appears more impressive; perhaps there is higher quality teaching. So find and exploit a USP!

1.03 ACCESS

Whatever the usp, your students must find access easy, travel cheap, accommodation affordable and the college must be close to public transport; the location must be safe, not threatening; there should be local shops, cafés, restaurants, not grimy factories nor anti-social environmental constructions.

1.04 APPEARANCE

The college should have a clear and identifiable 'presence' - it should not look like a sweetshop, a betting shop or a super market; it needs a degree of gravitas.

It is your aim to attract students to pay for something that, to be honest, can these days, be obtained more conveniently and at less cost via. the Internet or by home study. Your college, to justify the extra cost to the students, must add value to the learning experience. Degrees and certificates are available from a variety of sources so your college, its ambiance, teaching and environment, must be the 'value added', the reason why students do NOT take the learn-at-home option. There has to be something about the building that makes students want to attend. Therefore, attention to the external design within its location is vital.

The building should be near more than one form of public transport, near bus stops, underground and railway or tram routes. Ideally, for those with vehicles, it should provide free, safe parking. This easy access is also advantageous for delivery of college supplies and also for teaching and administrative staff. There should be local shops of all kinds and minimum noise and disturbance from construction work, traffic or groups of people.

The college should be a clearly identified with an obvious front entrance; everything should be clean and kept as new. First impressions are vital: you never get a second chance to make a first impression. The name of the college should be clearly stated as should its 'logo'.

Because your college is in competition with many others, it must have a clear and visible presence on the street, in the mall, or within the office block. To do this, select a **logo** or colour or shape and exploit it on the website; you need a separate entrance to your college on which your logo, colour or shape is prominent. This logo and colour scheme and perhaps an armorial design - a coat of arms - should be used in all college identification such as letter- heads, brochures, signage and all marketing and promotional material.

1.05 COLLEGE INCOME

This will probably come from 4 principle sources :

1.05.1 Fees from private students

1.05.2 Fees paid from Governmental or Local authority sources, either direct to the college or via. the students

1.05.3 Entrepreneurial or other income - from sponsorship, grants, research etc.
1.05.4 Fees paid by Local Governmental Agency for courses successfully bid for.

The fees from **private students** are a simple commercial negotiation; these fees are received direct from students or their families or sponsors to pay for the courses offered by the college. The college determines how much each student on each course must pay; this fee is to cover the college's teaching costs, overheads and a profit.

The college does not determine fees from **Governmental** or Local Authority sources; the Government negotiates a nationally agreed level of fees and that fee is what is paid on behalf of the student for the tuition provided. If the fee offered is less than the fee the college wishes or has to charge, then the student will have to make up the difference.

The third source is **entrepreneurial income**. Some colleges engage an entrepreneurial manager in the Marketing section. His job is to negotiate with external and commercial organisations to bring additional funding into the college. Such sources of income can include:

Product sponsorship: the college accepts a fee from (say) Coca-Cola for the installation of vending machines dispensing only products from that manufacturer.

Classrooms can be given names, sponsored by organisations that wish to place their name firmly in front of learners. One classroom could perhaps be named after a local manufacturer.

Another method is to link dissertation and research (for first and second degrees) with financial support from those companies who may benefit from receipt and analysis of the results.

If the college offers food and drink, this can be franchised to outside providers and the rental income and a share of the profit will be added to entrepreneurial income.

Bidding to run courses is a fourth way of obtaining funding. The college may decide to offer courses for which some form of governmentally - sourced payments are made direct to the college. In the case of many Higher Education awards, the fees are paid direct to the college. Such is the diversity of funding arrangement in Great Britain that there are many different ways in which courses offered by the college are paid for. One is to bid for funding. Here colleges devise courses and bid for the cost of providing a course from one of the many devolved government programmes.

This involves:

Identifying a need (often local and obscure)
Designing a course and (usually) offering a recognised award on completion
Structuring the delivery of the programme
Costing all aspects of the course : accommodation, development, management, monitoring and teaching.
Submitting a bid to the appropriate local funder.

This is time-consuming and has no guarantee of success. It is unrealistic to engage teachers and management and to make classrooms available until it is certain that funding will be provided for teaching the students. Other local colleges may compete for the limited funding available and usually the programme with the lowest cost for teaching each student receives the funding necessary to offer the course.

It is possible to negotiate to take over the delivery of a course from other local colleges who are already in receipt of funding for a course; they may be prepared to allow their students to attend but of course, they have already been the lowest bidder and so the amount they are prepared to pay your college will be even further reduced.

However, funding for courses is available and copies of typical documentation are included in **Appendix 2.**

There are other ways to obtain income and successful colleges constantly explore such opportunities.

It is advisable to divide the courses on offer between the private and publicly funded sectors.

1.06 COSTINGS

Appendix 11 shows a diagrammatic way to monitor and plot income against expenditure. It is essential to spend less than what is received; this surplus or profit can be re-invested or can provide for those periods when income is less than expected or to pay taxes legally demanded.

2] DESIGN AND ADMINISTRATION

"Design decisions : invested with values of truth, honesty and social advancement".
Bryan Appleyard (1986) (in the biography of Richard Rogers)

2.01 THE PSYCHOLOGY BEHIND THE DESIGN OF SPACES FOR LEARNING – HOW TO DESIGN A CLASSROOM THAT HELPS STUDENTS LEARN.

There is a direct relationship between the way teaching accommodation is designed and the way students learn best and this will be substantiated throughout. The accommodation is designed to facilitate the creation of an environment for learning in every way.

There are advantages in good environmental design, not only for the students, but for the college as well. Students studying in well-designed and attractive colleges with environmentally successful learning spaces achieve better exam results. If the college begins to achieve success, more motivated students are attracted to enrol. They will then achieve more exam success (especially in professional exams). This leads to the college attracting a higher number of student applications, the most highly motivated of whom can be selected for the college who, because of their motivation will achieve even more. In other words, success breeds success.

The most able and most dedicated students seek out the best colleges and their success attracts other equally motivated students. The publication and knowledge broadcast about the success of the students provides its own advertising and attracts a new influx of students. It can be possible to reduce the marketing spend as the college's achievements publicise themselves.

All college design should focus on student-centred learning which has these advantages; it allows the college to:

1. Encourage group bonding
2. Facilitate 'doing' not just 'listening'
3. Offer 1:1 tutorials
4. Permit students to learn at different speeds
5. Encourage more developed students to teach and guide others
6. Provide and support 'drop-in' facilities where students complete extra courses during less formal tuition periods
7. Utilise peer group pressure to foster harder work
8. Facilitate students to benefit from a wider range of experiences.
9. Work in groups, which emphasises bonding and problem solving; where cross-discipline subjects are integral, deeper thought processes are created.
10. Work with others because this represents real employment more accurately and also develops social skills.

The design of the classrooms, described in 2.02, is the logical place for student centred learning to be focused.

The learning environment is also designed as a response to student psychology, particularly the Hierarchy of Needs produced by **Maslow** in 1943. Maslow's hierarchy of needs is often depicted as a pyramid consisting of five levels: the four lower levels are grouped together as *deficiency needs* associated with physiological needs, while the top level is termed *growth needs* associated with psychological needs. This diagram appears in **Appendix 3.**

Deficiency needs must be met first. The higher needs in this hierarchy only come into focus when the lower needs in the pyramid are satisfied. Once an individual has moved upwards to the next level, needs in the lower level will no longer be prioritised. However, if a lower set of needs is no longer being met, the individual will temporarily re-prioritise those needs by focusing attention on the unfulfilled needs. The individual never regresses from one level to a lower one, however.

Deficiency needs

The first four layers of the pyramid are what Maslow called "deficiency needs" or "D-needs": the individual does not feel anything if they are met, but feels anxious and finds study harder, if they are not met. The deficiency needs are:

2.01.01 PHYSIOLOGICAL NEEDS LEVEL 1

The physiological needs take first precedence. These consist mainly of:

- Eating
- Drinking
- Sleeping
- Sex

If some needs are not fulfilled, a human's physiological needs take the highest priority. Physiological needs can control thoughts and behaviour, and can cause people to feel sickness, pain, and discomfort. Students cannot concentrate on their work for example if they are tired and hungry or have need of the lavatory.

2.01.02 SAFETY NEEDS LEVEL 2

When level 1 physiological needs are met, the need for safety will emerge. When one stage is fulfilled, a person naturally moves to the next. These include:

- Personal security from crime.
- Health and well-being
- Safety net against accidents/illness and the adverse impacts

Students who are concerned about the security of a family in an area where there is war will find focusing on lessons very difficult. They will also for example worry about leaving an expensive motor car parked near an area where it may be damaged or if they are concerned that they will be unable to fulfil their religious requirements and obligations. To ensure these are not a distraction or demotivator from learning, the college may want to provide safe parking and a prayer room.

2.01.03 LOVE / BELONGING / SOCIAL NEEDS LEVEL 3

After physiological and level 2 safety needs are fulfilled, the third layer of human needs is social. This aspect of Maslow's hierarchy involves emotionally based relationships in general, such as:

- friendship
- having a supportive and communicative family

Students need to feel a sense of belonging and acceptance, whether it comes from a social group (such as a club, culture, religious groups, professional organisations, sports teams, or small social connections or family members, intimate partners, mentors, close colleagues, confidants). They need to love and be loved by others. In the absence of these elements, many people become susceptible to loneliness, social anxiety, and depression. This need for belonging can often overcome the physiological and security needs, depending on the strength of the peer pressure. Students who worry, who are far from home and have yet to find friends, cannot study as well as those without such concerns. Many colleges provide trained councillors or allocate a teacher to talk over personal, non-academic worries students may have.

2.01.04 ESTEEM NEEDS LEVEL 4

All humans have a need to be respected, to have self-esteem, self-respect, and to respect others. People need to engage themselves to gain recognition and have an activity or activities that give a sense of contribution, to feel accepted and to be self-valued, perhaps in a profession or hobby. Imbalances at this level can result in low self-esteem and inferiority complexes. People with low esteem need respect from others and here the college and teachers can help.

However, confidence, competence and achievement only need one person and everyone else is inconsequential to one's own success. Many students with low self-esteem will not be able to improve their view of themselves simply by receiving fame, success or respect, but must first accept themselves internally. Psychological imbalances such as depression can also prevent students from obtaining self-esteem on both levels.

2.01.05 SELF-ACTUALISATION LEVEL 5

Self-actualisation is said to be the instinctive need of humans to make the most of their abilities and to strive to be the best they can. Maslow believed that humans have the need to increase their intelligence and thereby chase knowledge. Cognitive needs are the expression of the natural human need to learn, explore, discover and create to get a better understanding of the world around them.

In short, self-actualisation is reaching one's fullest potential. The students should always be encouraged to strive for this. This can affect the advice offered to and the course chosen by the students.

In addition Bruner (1960) suggested that the best way for students to learn about their subject, future career or profession was, in the absence of working in that profession, to write, speak, act and dress in that profession's fashion and style. He argues that:

> *"Intellectual activity anywhere is the same whether at the frontier of knowledge or in the classroom. What a scientist does at his desk or in his laboratory, what a literary critic does in reading a poem is of the same order as what anybody else does when he is engaged in like activities - if he is to achieve understanding. The difference is in degree, not in kind. The schoolboy learning physics is a physicist and it is easier for him to learn physics behaving like a physicist than doing something else. The something else usually involves the task of mastering...a middle language."*

By this Bruner claims that one of the keys to learning a subject is to use the verbal repertoire of that subject. Part of your task is to ensure that your learners acquire the knowledge to use the language of their subject. You help them by using and making them use the key vocabularies and behave appropriately and correctly.

To impress the essentiality of this, consider: if the students are being taught accountancy, where financial accuracy is important, then there must be no errors in their fee invoices; if they study English, there must be no spelling mistakes on college information. To complete Bruner's analysis, he suggests that Business Management students dress as managers (not students) and that Travel and Tourism students wear what travel agents or airline staff wear. The teachers will be appropriately dressed as well.

Equally students expect Financial and Management teachers to dress 'for the office' yet they perceive that IT professionals are often less formally dressed.

The application of these theories should be in evidence throughout college design and in environmental practices.

Some examples follow which combine the essentials from Maslow's hierarchy and these requirements should be built into the classroom design as identified in **2.02** below:

1. Temperature 18 - 20 degrees C - Maslow comfort needs. *Physiological*
2. Pinboard to display good work - Maslow need for praise. *Esteem*
3. Adjustable and non-rigid layout - to facilitate interaction. *Social*
4. Wipe clean surfaces - to avoid fear of mess being made and blame allocated. *Esteem*
5. Equipment and fittings - make sure it all works and is safe - Maslow security needs. *Safety*
6. Sound reverberation and absorption - students must be able to be confident they will be clearly heard. *Esteem*
7. Clocks - benefits of forewarning to identify time until a break in class. [this is explained further in the design of a lesson plan.] *Physiological*
8. Visibility - make students seem valued and important because praise equals improved response. *Esteem*
9. Seating – comfortable; classes may last 3 hours! *Physiological*
10. Colourful and patterned surfaces - these stimulate the right hand side of the brain. *Self-actualisation*

Further evidence of the importance of classroom design and the creation of a learning environment is offered by the success of Michel Thomas (born Moniek Kroskof in 1914) and whose life and work is comprehensively described by Solity (2008) and Robbins (2003). In his teaching, Thomas cleared classrooms of desks, and formal layout and introduced soft seating, planting and low level lighting. His language teaching made no use of books or writing yet his methods were outstandingly successful and not dissimilar to other, earlier teachers, Lozanov and Stevic who also removed teaching from the teacher-centred didactism of previous generations of teachers.

2.02 APPROVALS

Once the requirements and basic layout of the interior of the college have been designed and approved, attention can be drawn to the detailed **design** of the internal layout. Much of what is essential and is to be provided will be decided by the regulations of a local authority whose responsibility is to ensure that the work carried out is structurally safe, contains no hazardous materials and provides sufficient facilities for the people using the building. In Great Britain, local authorities will determine the number of toilets required, how in an emergency, safe escape from the building is carried out, the location of certain facilities, areas that require direct access to fresh external air and many other requirements. It is probably advisable to hire an architect or chartered building surveyor to produce detailed drawings for the approval of the local authority to ensure that all work is carried out to their requirements. If this is not done, local authorities have the power to order the work demolished and rebuilt to their satisfaction.

2.03 CLASSROOMS

The classrooms should be seen as the place for and belonging to the student; students must not have the feeling that they 'are playing away from home' as this will restrict their learning.

In the **classrooms,** focus should be on contemporary learning methodology incorporated into classroom design. This means that the classrooms should have attractive ambience, clear sight lines from seating to whiteboard / screen / plasma TV, sound absorption materials on the walls to prevent sound pollution from adjacent rooms. It may be advisable to engage an architect or surveyor to specify what is required.

Technological aids should be provided to allow the students the most up-to-date visual learning opportunities with video, cd etc.

Teachers should use *coloured* pens on whiteboards; colours, shapes and diagrams used together are more useful as memory aids than black and white writing - more areas of the brain are stimulated. Notice boards, for the display of good work as well as information, should be fixed to most walls at eye level. This provides visual stimulus, competition and proof of reward for good work, all psychological attributes to learning. Teachers should be offered choices in the arrangements of seating. At times learners will work in groups close together; at other times, teaching in a semi-circle may be more appropriate so the seating and writing facilities need to be easily adjustable and flexible and this may influence the choice of what to purchase. It may be suitable to provide desks and chairs but alternatives include chairs with wide arms on which to write. If this form of seating is chosen ensure that at least 15% of the chairs are suitable for those who write with their left hand.

To maximise flexibility, some classrooms will have desks, others will have chairs with armrests, and others simply chairs. The Director of Studies will be aware of the demands of the options to be employed by teachers in each of their lessons and will allocate the classroom laid out most appropriately.

The position of the teacher and seated learners is important; a fixed desk separates the teacher behind it from the learners in front of it. It forms a barrier between teacher and learner and discriminates. Is this what is wanted? Does it impede the relationship between teacher and learners? Again depending on the knowledge of the teacher and Director of Studies, when planning the allocation of rooms, students of certain cultural backgrounds actually prefer a formal approach.

There are some cultures where inter-action with the teacher is not usual; students from some cultures demand to 'sit at the feet' of professors and expect a 'lecture' with minimum of interaction and in these cases, desks, lecterns or a teaching dais are not unusual nor abnormal but expected; they show, in some cultures, an inherent formal relationship between the teacher and the taught. Early negation of this can lead to student discord and confusion.

There should be natural light, fresh air, and in cold or hot weather appropriate temperature control. The heating source must not be intrusive because fan heaters in cold weather and noisy, oscillating fans in hot weather can disturb student concentration.

Make it possible to darken the classrooms so that TV, video, overhead projector pictures or slides can be clearly seen. This system should be simple to operate, speedy, and effective.

The surfaces in the classroom should be durable and be constructed of material so that walls and floors are easily and quickly wiped or washed clean every evening as identified in **6.08**.

OTHER STUDENT AREAS

2.04 CIRCULATION SPACES throughout the college should be uniform, colour coded, with unambiguous signage, presenting a constant image; there should be **notice boards**, one for each of the faculties or awarding bodies whose courses are offered so that students know where they will find information about the courses they are taking. The must be **toilets** which are adequate in number and separate for male and female, with electric hand-dryers (to abolish paper waste), infra-red activated taps (to save water) mirrors, and a separate supply of drinking water here and throughout the college. As well as classrooms there will need to be **testing rooms** for assessing student ability although these can have other uses such as interview rooms when new students arrive.

2.05 LECTURE THEATRES / HALLS

Depending on the number of enrolled students and their timetabling and with the opportunity to host degree and other award ceremonies, it may be decided to dedicate part of the college to a lecture theatre or hall. This choice may necessitate reducing other spaces to allow this one function. Prospective students and their fee-paying parents or sponsors may be impressed with the ability to hold prestigious gatherings - such as prize-giving ceremonies - within the college itself and the costs of hiring an external location for ceremonies is avoided.

The space itself can also serve for 'guest' lectures where college students gather to listen to an outside speaker whose content crosses the boundaries of several disciplines. For financial reasons it can be advantageous to economise on cost with one lecturer / guest being able to lecture to a large number of students at the same time; this provides cost compensation for the small groups of students who receive, seminars or tutorials or even 1:1 tuition.

This space, able to accommodate upwards of one hundred people, needs be larger in volume and with higher ceilings than classrooms; for this reason, a decision to include a lecture theatre is one that is made early in the college design process. It may be necessary to incorporate changes in floor level so that those further back can still view the speaker. In addition, it provides opportunities, if included from the beginning, to include contemporary multi-media facilities such as TV screen projection / plasma screen behind the speaker. It also allows clear presentation of visual aids; it allows for the acoustics to be designed so that amplified sound is adequately provided throughout with no distortion; plasma screens can be built into each seat back into which images from the large plasma projection screen, videos, slides or diagrams can be provided. The seat backs themselves contain fold-out A4 note pad holders for each student. A design for seating in a lecture hall is included in **Appendix 4.**

Such a space can become an asset to the college if designed properly and if timetabled into use. It allows examinations for large groups of students to be held with minimal supervision in a controlled environment at the same time. This allows the classrooms to be used for other purposes.

There is the opportunity to rent out fully fitted lecture theatres to external organisations who need to provide 'training' for staff or for meetings in general. Therefore the implementation of a lecture theatre within the college can become revenue producing. However its inclusion must be decided at the design stage, so it must be fully costed, fully fitted out and made good use of.

2.06 ADMINISTRATIVE STAFF FACILITIES – SPACE REQUIREMENTS

Depending on the number of students, sufficient space for office staff will be needed and it is essential that adequate **desk space** be allowed for this. Modern administrative staff also known as admin. staff require space on a desk for a computer, screen, keyboard, perhaps a printer, layout space and drawers for storing information and adjacent filing cabinets. It is probable that admin. staff will spend a considerable time in interviews and discussions with individual students and with teachers so separate seating and layout facilities next to the work-station are essential. Do not underestimate the space needed for admin. staff members and allow for adequate circulation space around them. For these reasons an 'L-shaped' workspace is often found to be suitable. The electrical provision to service each admin. space is also a requirement. 3 double switch socket outlets is a reasonable capacity to provide at each space. Telephone and broadband connexions are essential and intranet (internal college messaging) will also be provided.

The admin. office itself, in addition to desks for staff, will require storage facilities (for all general filing and storage) reproduction facilities, availability for safe storage of additional technology aids such as tape recorder, cd player video camera and other teaching aids etc.

2.07 MANAGEMENT STAFF FACILITIES

Separate offices are required for senior staff with which can be combined some element of storage; there will be an office for the following:

Principal
Vice-principal
Director of Studies
Bursar
Marketing department

Predominantly these offices are needed to guarantee privacy and confidentiality and to allow meetings of relevant groups of staff to take place. In addition, confidential spaces are required for meetings with external examiners, awarding bodies, inspectorates et al. For these reasons, one of the offices, perhaps that of the principal, should be large enough to accommodate about 15 people around a conference table.

One of the offices should contain a secure safe for examination papers and answer scripts.

2.08 RECEPTION,

A reception area should be located adjacent to the admin. office. This should be cheery and welcoming with an area for talking to students and space for form filling. Often this is the first stop for students joining or thinking of joining the college so it is the first and last chance to impress and encourage them. Make time for a new face - identify and remember the students' names and origin; offer them refreshment (if appropriate) because this student may be one who moves through the college, first learning English, then taking a diploma then a degree and spending 5 years of fee-paying time with you. Help the student to fill in forms and offer as much assistance as you can; moving to another city or another country or just moving into another environment (full or part-time study rather than work) is a big and challenging step; help as much as you can.

You need to include a separate and private space where teachers and admin. staff can talk to students although it is inadvisable to close the door entirely even if there are sight-lines through a window out of the room. This precaution is to minimise the remote possibility of a student making a false accusation about improper behaviour.

Never minimise what, to the student is a problem, but offer to find a solution. The solution may be the reason why the student selects your college from others and may have nothing to do with educational credibility. Often of course the student wants sympathy and understanding not a solution.

OTHER ADMIN. FACILITIES

2.09 COMMON ROOM. When not at their desk admin. staff and teaching staff require space for break time where lunch can be eaten, papers read and where conversation can take place. This common room should be separate from the admin. office spaces and separate from any student leisure facilities and should have easy chairs, a desk and facilities for refreshments with a water supply, sink and kettle and a refrigerator.

2.10 TOILET FACILITIES These staff facilities should be separate from those of the students if possible.

2.11 REPRODUCTION FACILITIES, photocopiers and printers are nowadays cheap and simple to use; basic models are needed in several locations so that certificates, letters etc. can quickly be copied; a larger model(s) is required for large volume copying of texts, circulars, student handouts etc. This should be located somewhere separate from general office use and separate from printing facilities from the office computers, so for them, another printer(s) is needed.

DATA STORAGE FACILITIES

2.12 HARD COPY AND COMPUTER FILING SYSTEMS; obviously a college needs an up to date fully functional management information system; on this (and backed up!) are stored programs to record:

teaching staff details
student details
payments due for course fees
courses
contact details
attendance records
students' marks for examinations, course work tests etc.

Admin. staff and programme managers require computer access to record student class lists and record timetable details and monitor student attendances - a requirement of government and local authorities in Great Britain who need to verify that students from other countries actually do attend class and are genuine students as explained further in **6.04**.

IT Manager. Unless a staff member [perhaps an IT lecturer] is qualified in IT management and is happy and available to rectify, adapt, install and upgrade computer programs, an IT manager or technician must be engaged. *Computer maintenance* is a vital part of the college strength; there must be continuous access to records, databases, e-mail etc. He can be full or part-time or an outside consultant. He will require a workroom and storage facilities for obsolete machinery and new equipment, hardware and software.

Separately the **bursar** requires access to programs updating monies in and out, highlighting defaults, imminent payments etc. so that at any time the overall financial picture of the college can be presented to those who need to know it.

Marketing requires facilities to record and analyse success rates in advertising placed and responses generated. [see **chapter 8.00**]

Teachers / examiners / markers require access to computers to check evidence and to run anti-plagiarism programmes. They also require co-ordination with the admin. staff's class lists to enable marks / grades to be exchanged.

Publications on country requirements, academic equivalences: be aware of the inter-relationship of different countries' academic standards so that the validity of students' home-acquired certificates and diplomas can be quickly checked on line or in published form.

2.13 ANCILLARY AREAS

In addition to offices, ancillary space needs to be provided for

Cleaning staff storage
Archive storage
Toilet / hygiene pre-requisites
Hot and cold water storage

ANCILLARY STUDENT FACILITIES

2.14 IT FACILITIES AND COMPUTERS with collection of interactive dvds;

Students learn at different speeds and within the extensive syllabus may choose to explore various aspects. It is also unreasonable to expect that teachers will be always available for advice or guidance. In addition, for economic reasons, there is a college requirement for students, at times, to learn on their own.

Computer suites comprise individual spaces in which a computer, screen and keyboard are installed. Tuition like this can be expensive to set up (and update!) but once installed it is cheap to operate and can fulfil some of the tasks of expensive teachers. Each computer is connected to the mainframe and via. intranet to all other computers throughout the college.

Students provide their own disks / memory sticks on which they store their work; they can access or borrow programs in which they are interested and can access the intranet for specific college information. Colleges can supply assignments, deadline dates and handouts on the intranet for student use. Students can then work at their own speed, accumulating and saving appropriate information. The necessary computer and keyboard skills are assumed but refresher courses in elementary computing skills should be available in the college at regular intervals and such tuition would be an essential part of a foundation or first year study skills course.

Wireless access should be available throughout the college for those students bringing in their own lap-top computers.

This computer suite should be provided with up to date pcs, broadband enabled, with password access for every student, to allow free access to the internet and e-mail. Dvds for study use should be available to enable students to learn at their own speed to supplement classroom learning and to enable coursework, assignments and homework to be completed. The college should subscribe to an appropriate range of data base web sites. Some business - based sites are listed below.

ProQuest which is an on-line database that gives access to articles in over eight hundred journals back to 1991 and an additional seven hundred journals dating from 1971 onwards

Business Source Complete which provides full text for more than 3,650 scholarly business journals, including nearly 1,100 peer-reviewed publications relating to business as far back as the year 1922

Fame which gives detailed financial data for over half a million British companies; ownership and descriptive information for an additional 1.3 million companies in the UK and Ireland, and which also includes global industries' profiles

Nexis UK which is a business intelligence service which includes newspapers, wire services, market research and country reports, corporate profiles, government documents and legislation and case law for the UK and Europe

Mintel Oxygen which offers analysis of market size and trends, market segmentation, consumer behaviour and future market developments and changes

Emerald Xtra which includes articles from 410 journals at the heart of business & management. It also provides 700 cases studies and 400 literature reviews.

2.15 LIBRARY: with seating and lay-out tables for study facilities; a wide stock of books covering the spread of subjects offered at the college is needed. There should be multiple copies of which one copy should always be 'reference' and is not to be borrowed. A 'Dewey system' of referencing should be utilised or one based on subject heads, if the spread of courses is deliberately restricted. Books need to be electronically protected to prevent theft and a system of fines for late return introduced to assist in circulating the stock. Depending on the size of the college, a librarian or dedicated admin. staff member should oversee the library when open and should be familiar with issue and receipt of borrowed books.

The Dewey system classifies books offering unique number to each. The Dewey system is shown in **Appendix 5.**

Often students are encouraged to assist in the running of the library.

OTHER DESIRABLE STUDENT FACILITIES

2.16 RELIGIOUS REQUIREMENTS

Prayer rooms / dedicated spaces for religious worship; where it is expected that students may have firm religious beliefs and obligations, it can be sensible to provide somewhere for their duties to be carried out; this obviates the need for them to leave the building and is often a persuasive factor in encouraging such students to select your college.

2.17 VICTUALS

A **café** can provide students with the opportunity to waste less time when hungry but it can also provide an income to the college. If sufficient numbers warrant it, a café / brasserie can be franchised; an outside organisation will pay a rental and a share of the profits to the college in return for providing food and drink to a captive market - the staff and students.

If possible, provide a separate recreation space in the college where students can inter-act; provide desks and chairs. If there is external space, provide a secure and safe 'garden' where students can walk and talk – and smoke cigarettes!

2.18 DOCUMENTATION

The effective management of the college still depends on keeping records and much of this is still paper-based. There follows a list of required documentation, essential for effective administration and required evidence for any accreditation that may be sought. These documents are often stored electronically (with manual back-up) and are managed by dedicated members of the administrative team under the guidance of the Vice Principal. Expansion of the purpose of these documents and an explanation of their function is found in **6.02**

Company Accounts
The Bursar will maintain a copy of the last three years' accounts for inspection when legally required.

Premises and Health and safety
Floor Plans of the College
Insurance Certificates
Health and Safety documentation showing all compliances
Fire precaution provision and a fire risk assessment; means of escape diagrams
Necessary planning, Building Regulations and Environmental Health Approvals
Records of fire alarm practice and evacuation drills

Management and Staff Resources
Diagram of staffing structure (see example in **Chapter 6**)
List of names and designations of staff
CVs of management, academic and senior staff (and passport / visa evidence of their entitlement to remain in UK)
Staff appointment procedure and sample advertisements
Staff contracts
Equal Opportunities policy
Staff handbook
Procedures for recording student attendance, monitoring and taking action
Procedures for examinations
Procedures for the production of examination papers

Arrangements for the secure storage of examination papers and examination scripts
Minutes of Staff meetings and academic boards,
Evidence that staff qualifications have been verified

Teaching and Learning
Student application form
Pre-enrolment information for students dealing with course entry requirements, fees payable, documents required etc.
Student handbook
Course timetables showing minimum 15 contact hours / week for each course
Course descriptions
Course curricula, syllabi, course programmes
Learning outcomes, aims and objectives
Samples of marked student work
Sample lesson plans
Emergency lesson plans
Evidence of balanced work-load for students
Sample examination papers

Quality Control
Quality handbook / manual
Records of meetings relating to curriculum development, course design, course review
Course approval documentation (for internally designed courses)
Documentation confirming the level of courses internally designed and offered (for example IELTS 5.5)
Records of student assessment (formal / informal; actual, predictive etc)
Student course evaluation forms
Records of meetings involving students
Procedure for selection of student representatives
Staff development policy
Staff appraisal records
Teacher monitoring forms
Staff warning letters
Job Descriptions
Person Specifications

Student Welfare
Pre-arrival information for International students about life in UK
Meet and greet service and costs.
Accommodation service

Awards and Qualifications
Details of each course offered
Guidance on academic misconduct
Evidence of formal arrangements and procedures in place with awarding bodies, university partners etc.
Examination boards – minutes, mark sheets etc.

Marketing and Student recruitment
Ethics policy
Criteria for the appointment of agents
Agency agreement
Briefing document for agents
Prospectus
Procedures for processing enquiries and applications
Procedures relating to student admission and enrolment
Procedures for monitoring students' academic progress
Procedures for handling deposits, fee payments and refunds
Press cuttings

Relationship with Governmental Offices and reporting mechanisms
Student attendance records - registers
Sample letters to students about absences
Sample letters to students about non-enrolment
Sample letters to Home Office about student absence
Sample letters to Home office about student non-enrolment.
Student files with passport, visa and previous qualification details

3] STUDENTS

"I don't know the key to success but the key to failure is to try to please everyone." Bill Cosby (1937-)

3.01 Enrolment
3.02 Retention
3.03 Status
3.04 Social facility

For a private college, dependence on non-English or non-governmentally funded fee payers requires a different approach to one where the Government funds the majority of students.

In the former, fees can be set by what the client will pay; in the second case, there is often a maximum fee that is funded by governmental or local authorities. College stakeholders will decide what types are expected to be in the majority, the structure of the college and the courses and qualifications on offer. This will be decided on the basis of whether or not the guarantees of government funding of lower cost courses will be more attractive than the higher fees from private students. Often government-funded students are local to the college and speak the native language sufficiently well to undertake study. Therefore, if it is expected that students already have a good knowledge of English, then the college can focus more on offering higher-level courses - diplomas and degrees - where support courses in Study Skills are more important than support in English.

The difference is fundamental; the college must decide to what extent English language will be a part of the syllabus and this applies predominantly when the college enrols students whose first language is not English. With these students, the college should develop an approach where courses lead from lower level English to Masters degrees.

Therefore, the college needs to decide the focus of students to be enrolled. Often this can be a financial decision; students studying for Degrees and Higher-Level qualifications pay higher fees than those studying for Certificate and English Language courses although it is the hope that their success in these will convince them to continue their studies at a higher level.

3.01 ENROLMENT

The procedure for enrolling any level of student is a process that needs to be carefully planned. There are fundamental obligations on the college. These are:

- To explain clearly how much and when payment is required from the student to the college.
- To minimise any risk of quasi students entering the UK whose intention is either to cause a drain on the public purse or to attempt illegal action.
- To ensure that monies held on behalf of the student - for application, for fees or for extra charges - are always allocated for the appropriate purpose; tracking the finances must be easy, transparent and honest.

3.01.01 ADMISSION

Admission to college courses is usually made through the administrative office whose staff consider experience and skills alongside formal qualifications. Such considerations must reflect what is published on the college website and in the prospectus. This opens admission to students unable to offer formal qualifications but whose motivation demonstrates a willingness to learn. Such students also need to show understanding of the aims of a proposed course of study, provide reports from referees, and sometimes need to offer further information which can be just as important as qualifications.

You may decide to accept students for entry at each stage of the college year, during any of the 2 or 3 college terms or semesters. If many of the courses run throughout the year, students can join their chosen course of study on any of 3 separate dates. The structure of the college year, the allocation of courses within the term or semester programme and the availability of courses within each is the responsibility of the Director of Studies working in conjunction with the Principal. It is an administrative responsibility on which the success of the college can depend. Students entering at certain times must be certain that their lack of knowledge about a course or subject offered earlier in the college year, does not preclude them from achieving.

Students from various backgrounds who can demonstrate real enthusiasm and are ready to get on with real life challenges are enrolled on professional courses. There should be no official deadlines for forwarding an application for admission, but students should apply several weeks before the course commencement date. Admission should be confirmed within two weeks after the application is received. Students seeking to join the college should be expected to follow a procedure similar to the following.

3.01.02 DOCUMENTS REQUIRED

A completed application form which should be available from the website and submitted with a non-refundable registration fee.

Other important documents include :

A certified copy of all academic and professional awards and transcripts (in their original language). Documents other than English language must be translated. The value of these qualifications is verified by checking. (see **2.12**)

Originals of IELTS / TOEFL scores, if English is not the student's first language (copies are not usually acceptable)

An official recommendation letter from previous institution, if attended, or from the employer, if previously employed.

A copy of the passport or an original letter of immigration (applicable to international students only); an up to date visa if already in the applicant's possession.

Original sponsorship certificates are required from the respective authorities where a sponsor pays the student fees.

3.01.02 A STUDENTS ENTERING UK COLLEGES UNDER THE POINTS BASED SYSTEM -TIER 4

From **March 2009**, colleges who want to be able to sponsor potential students from outside the European Economic Area [EEA] must possess a **sponsor licence**. This is obtained from the UK Border Agency. Student visa applications will be refused if the college is not licensed and entered on the Sponsor register.

The students themselves must show that they have sufficient funds to pass a maintenance test (enough money to live on) and must possess proof of a previous level of education that fits them to begin the course for which they have applied.

The college will provide a Confirmation of Acceptance of Studies [CAS] when offering a place to an applicant from outside the EEA and it is this document that will be needed for the visa application. The applicant will also require a letter from the college fully detailing the course of study to be undertaken. This letter must include the following :

The would-be student's name, nationality and address in the country of permanent residence. The licence number of the college, the sponsor. Course title. Course start date. Expected course end date. List of documents used by the college to assess academic ability to complete the course . The student's passport number.

Full details are available on : www.ukba.homeoffice.gov.uk

In brief, without a sponsor licence the college cannot recruit students from outside the EEA. With a sponsor licence, all details identified above are required to enable to student to obtain a visa to enter the UK. From 2010, the system goes on line with greater requirements.

3.01.03 ENTRY QUALIFICATIONS

An offer of a place will generally be based on a combination of examination passes, and where appropriate, passes at specific grades in specific subjects are required in order to ensure that students have the background knowledge and general ability required to cope with the demands of their chosen course.

3.01.04 HOW THE APPLICATION IS PROCESSED

When applications are received, the administrative office will forward them to an Admission Committee, a group of lecturers, admin staff and the Vice-Principal. After due consideration of the application one of the following three actions will be taken. The college will:

i. Make the student an unconditional offer, or
ii. Make the student a conditional offer which will require achievement of further qualifications before admission, or
iii. Decline the application this time

3.01.05 OVERSEAS ENTRY REQUIREMENTS

All students should fulfil the entry qualifications. The details of the recognised international qualifications or their equivalents will be checked beforehand.

3.01.06 ENGLISH LANGUAGE REQUIREMENTS

Candidates whose first language is not English must show ability by attaining an acceptable English language qualification before they can be admitted onto some courses although the college may already offer tuition in English as a Foreign language. (See **Appendix 9** where the range of awards and levels are shown)

3.01.07 OTHER REQUIREMENTS

The college may wish to implement other requirements and qualifications such as:

- New students are permitted to register for courses on a first-come, first-served basis.
- All applicants must satisfy the college's basic admission requirements and must meet other admission criteria as may be stipulated by the admission committee.
- With the development of the internet and e-mail, it is now more usual for enquiries and applications to initially be made on line with postal confirmation of required documentation submitted later.

Prospective students should be reminded of the following

a) Applications for admission must be accessed, completed and submitted online or by post.
b) Applications with missing information, without the application fee or received closer than 6 weeks before course commencement will not always be processed in time, so students should not make firm travel arrangements.
c) Applicants must arrange to have all official final transcripts and other supporting documentation where applicable, delivered to the Admissions Office by a deadline date.

3.01.08 THE APPLICATION FORM

All students filling in the Application Form by hand should do it carefully according to instructions provided in the form, clearly stating everything, by filling all the sections applicable and the writing must be clear and legible, using, if hand written, capital letters in black ink. The same detail is required when completing an application form on line. The completed Application Form must be sent with the following documents:

a) Three (3) passport size (colour) photographs.
b) The Registration Fee (the registration fee is not refundable)
c) All relevant certificate and documents (either original or attested or verified by the proper authorities)
d) Photocopies of relevant sections of the passport

Applicants should be informed that a completed Application Form sent without the fee and documents cannot be processed.

3.01.09 BEFORE EVALUATION

Within 1-2 business days, the college should send an e-mail to the student confirming receipt of the application and issuing a unique College Identification Number and stating any other information that may be necessary to process the application for admission.

3.01.10 EVALUATION OF APPLICATION

When all documents in support of an application are received, the Admin Office will evaluate the student's academic record to determine if the basic faculty / programme admission criteria have been satisfied in accordance with the admission criteria. The faculty / programme may require additional criteria to be satisfied so students should be reminded of these criteria which are to be completed by the specified deadline dates.

Where applicable, a meeting of the Admissions Board is held to consider these applications and make decisions about admission. The Admissions Board should also calculate whether or not there are sufficient students about to be enrolled so that each advertised course programme can be taught.

Students should be informed that they will be considered for their first programme choice and may be offered admission. If an offer of admission is not given for the first programme of choice, depending on other academic abilities, the applicant may be placed on a waiting list until it can be determined if there is availability.

Offers of admission will be made as quickly as possible and continuously throughout the year. Any final decisions will also be conveyed in writing by e-mail and post. To assist international students applying from outside the UK they will normally not be placed on a waiting list. Instead, they will automatically be offered their second choice of study.

Upon receipt of the completed Application Form, all other related documents and registration fees, the College will process the Application Form and if successful, the College will issue an **Acceptance letter**. (see.**3.01.02A**)

The Acceptance letter will offer a place on the students' choice of course and subject. Students will be asked how payment of the tuition fees is to be made. Students should sign the Acceptance letter in order to accept the place and send it back.

When the college receives the signed Acceptance letter and agreement about payment of tuition fees, the college will confirm that a place has been reserved on the course. Overseas students may use the Acceptance letter to obtain a student entry visa to the UK from the UK Embassy / High Commission / British Council in their own country. Students to be funded by the government or local authority can use the letter to apply for grants and loans.

Once a place is offered by the College and accepted by the candidate, the college is encouraged to require payment of one half of the tuition fees before the enrolment letter is sent. For overseas students, full payment of the fees may be required. Students can be advised that this payment shows good faith and confirms the place and that failure to make the payment may result in loss of admission. The bursar who can also offer the options for making the actual payment sends this letter. He can also offer to provide a flexible payment scheme for students who may have financial difficulties. Any such arrangements must be within the requirements of Tier 4 student sponsorship, the need for the provision of funds for maintenance during the course.

It should be explained that for some courses, books and material costs, may be included with the course fees, but for many courses, students are expected to buy their own books and materials. The college must make this all information clear during enrolment.

The college must also advise students that any students who fail their exams and have to repeat a course will be asked to pay the fees again in full.

All fees to UK colleges are payable in GBP by:

- Cash
- Personal Cheque
- Bank Transfer
- IMO [International Money Order](for overseas students only)

Many banks now offer Direct Bank Transfer for which the college must publish the following:

Number of College Bank Account; Sort code number; Title of Account; Bank and Bank Address; IBAN number; [International Bank Account Number] a BIC Bank Identification Code. This ensures direct inter-currency transfers within 3 or 4 days at low cost.

The College may impose an interest charge on any unpaid tuition fees, which will be waived *only* after valid reasons are found for late payment and when evidence is provided.

3.01.11 REFUND POLICY AND COURSE WITHDRAWAL

For all overseas students, a refund of tuition deposit but not the application fee will be made *only if* an entry visa to UK is refused by the appropriate UK authority and if the original refusal documents, including copies of all the pages of the passport and original Letter of Admission and all other documents are sent to the college. If this procedure is correctly followed, the college is obliged to refund the entire amount of deposited course fees to an overseas student. Students who are already in the UK may qualify for a refund of tuition fees but the refund will be made in accordance with the following guiding rules:

- Students seeking a refund should, in either case, should apply in writing to the Administrative Officer of the College and explain the reasons for seeking a refund.
- Documentary evidence should be provided, where applicable
- To get 90% fees refund, withdrawal of a course must be notified in writing two weeks before the course commencement date.

- As part of the procedure, students are required to submit list of reasons why they have to withdraw from the course.
- Only 50% fees refund will be made, if a course withdrawal letter with no valid reason is sent to the college within four (4) weeks of course commencement date.
- No refund will be made after the fourth week
- Refund will only be made payable to the original payee by cheque
- No refund will be made if a student enters the UK on a student visa obtained on the basis of the college's letters of acceptance and enrolment.
- No refund is permitted or shall be made when a student decides to leave the college for whatever reason after the issue of or visa or the subsequent extension of a student visa obtained through the college's facilitation.
- The college has an obligation to notify the Government if a student is issued with a student visa on the basis of an acceptance letter and does not attend college to enrol.

3.01.12 REGISTRATION WITH THE UNIVERSITY/AWARDING BODY

Some course programmes require the students to register with and pay a fee to the University / Awarding Body from which they will get the Degree, Certificate or Diploma.

For the course programmes which require the students to register with them, it is the responsibility of all students concerned to do so and to register with the University / awarding body at their own cost and by the appropriate time. The college will assist in every way possible.

Students should be informed that registration with your college is separate from the registration with that of the University / Awarding Institution.

3.01.13 TERMS AND CONDITIONS APPLICABLE

The college should make the following clear to all prospective students

The college reserves the right to make any changes at any time regarding admission requirements, fees, policies, tuition, rules and regulations and academic programme before the course programme starts.

Enrolment for a course, together with the payment of the required deposit, creates a binding agreement to follow the course and to pay the full fees.

The registration fee is non refundable.

The College reserves the right to cancel any advertised courses because of insufficient number of students. In such a situation, the fees paid will be refunded, unless the student concerned chooses an alternative course programme.

The college may refund tuition fees paid in advance only if an international student shows the visa application has been refused. In this case, original documents must be submitted. If these documents are submitted after commencement of the course, the first term's fees may be deducted.

No refunds are due if the overseas student has already arrived in the UK and has chosen not to join the course after its commencement.

The College has the right to take action against any student because of poor attendance, absenteeism or violation any of the regulations concerning class attendance.

Anyone supplying false information in the Application Form is liable to face suspension from the college.

The College reserves the right to require a student to leave a course at any stage if the student does not fulfil the above requirements or if a student's continued presence would, in the opinion of the college, be detrimental to the well-being of the staff, other students or the college generally or if a student does not meet his or her financial obligations. Any fees paid by the student will not be refunded if such an action would require the student to leave the college.

The College reserves the right to place a student on to a course starting at future date if the student arrives late for his course without reasonable excuse.

The college reserves the right to take any decision at any time regarding its policies and / or amend regulations and the decision of the College administration must be treated as final.

3.01.14 COMPLIANCE WITH UK HOME OFFICE REGULATIONS

The college staff and the prospective students should be aware of the following.

The UK Home Office / Border Agency has published strict legal measures for international students seeking higher education in UK. The following are important guidelines that all students ought to adhere to in order for further leave to remain in the UK for the purpose of study.

Students must enrol as full time on British recognised programmes or professional courses. Students should not engage in courses (certificate, diplomas & language programmes) lower than degree level for more than two years, unless undertaking a professional course lasting for more than two years such as ACCA, accountancy qualifications.

While studying, students must maintain more that 80% class attendance for taught courses. Attendance below 80% is acceptable only in exceptional cases when documentary evidence can be provided to satisfy UK Home Office authorities of the reasons for failure to maintain the required level of attendance.

Communication by e-mail, telephone and warning letters for non-attendance will be sent as follows:

- 1st letter – after one week's absence
- 2nd letter – after 2 weeks absence and no response
- 3rd letter – after 3 weeks absence, no response and terminating the registration of the student and with a letter to the Home Office. This will invalidate the student's visa.

Progress in course work should be made at each level, as the progress report of the previous year is required by the Home Office for granting a visa extension.

Students are only allowed to work part time during term time; however, there will be no problem in working full time during semester breaks and during vacations.

Students who are Commonwealth nationals may be eligible for short-term (six months) permission to remain in the UK. During the stay, students should be able to change their visa status to student, only if they enrol on a degree level recognised course in a bona fide institute of learning.

Further changes in UK regulations concerning overseas students occur regularly in order to ensure that students pursue their studies systematically and in time without causing recourse to public resources. The latest information is available at www.ind.homeoffice.gov.uk. The college requires its students to strictly adhere to the UK immigration rules and UK Home Office regulations for overseas students.

3.02 RETENTION

Once the students enrol for any course, it should be easier to retain them and encourage them to continue to take additional and higher level courses. There needs to be a series of inducements to encourage students to continue at the college so inducements to continue must be prepared. Incentives can be offered and these are developed in Chapter 8 Marketing

3.03 STATUS

Often students at colleges in UK come from relatively wealthy families abroad and are often accustomed to a higher standard of living and a more luxurious quality of life. Therefore, the change engendered by the move to a more cost effective way of life can be stressful. College management needs to understand that this can be difficult. The daily and weekly need to part with real but different currency is often unusual for some students; they may be used to being able to do what they want to do when they want to do it. Prohibition on smoking, spitting, shouting, wearing headgear and other idiosyncrasies can often be unexpected and reinforcement of the college rules initially needs to be gentle and with explanations given.

3.04 SOCIAL FACILITY

Your college is the students' 'home from home' during their stay so apart from the provision of superb facilities for learning and study, the college should offer 'extra-mural' activities to unite students from disparate locations, cultures and creeds.

The college should be able to provide easy access to a list of facilities that are asked for by most students; there must be available contacts for students who want to take part in:

Sports
Theatre
Cinema
Religious worship
Cultural roots

Travel throughout UK and Europe
Additional studies
Membership of professional organisations (British Library, Management organisations etc)

3.05 STUDENT NAMES.

Frequently students from Asia choose to use names they consider 'more English' as Chinese and Japanese names are often similar, possess in-built meanings and are thought unsuitable. However often the chosen names are equally unsuitable being selected from out of date English language text books.

Be prepared for female students to choose to be called *Fanny, Gay* or *Esmeralda.* Male students often choose *Elvis.*

3.06 SKYPE

With modern internet technology, it is now easy to interview foreign students 'face to face'; the computer manager should be responsible for installing the appropriate software and for ensuring the equipment – camera, microphone etc – are always in good working order. All appropriate staff should be trained in the use of Skype (or similar).

4] COURSES

"Little minds are interested in the extraordinary; great minds in the commonplace."
Elbert Hubbard (1856-1915)

4.01 Short term
4.02 Medium
4.03 Long term
4.04 Level : low – high

Students will enrol for courses of all lengths and durations subject to the regulations explained in 3.10.14; English language courses usually offer courses of approximately 4/6 weeks to move students from one level to the next - Intermediate to upper-intermediate for example. [530 to 600 ToEFL]

In order to enrol, register, teach, test and provide accommodation for a student for only a few weeks involves as much administrative work as if the student was enrolling for a 3-year degree programme. So although frequent, short courses can, if full of block-booked students, contribute to the income of the college, but they can become expensive to organise, plan and run.

Obviously, a college concentrating only on short-term students has high administrative costs and may find difficulty in attracting students because of the level of fees that must be charged. It is easier to combine short, medium and long-term courses in order to dissipate the administrative work.

A **short** course lasts from 2 to 6 weeks: English language

A **medium length** course is one or two terms – 12 to 24 weeks: Certificate

A **long** course is from 1 year upwards: Diploma (1 year) Degree 2 / 3 years

4.01 SHORT COURSES

A short course lasts from 2 to 6 weeks and a typical language course fulfils this requirement; students may continue from the lowest language level to the highest, from Elementary [300 ToEFL] to Advanced [670+] and this journey, where each increment takes about 6 weeks, will last for more than 30 weeks or the majority of an academic year. The agreed stages of English language learning are shown in **Appendix 9**.

For long-stay English language students, although paying relatively low fees, they are less of a burden on the administration because they have only one contact address and one accommodation, one registration and one mentor. It is expected that as they progress in their knowledge of English language there will be opportunities to guide them onto low level academic courses, suitable for improving their level of English. For this, additional fees will be attracted. It is considered good academic practice-and sound financial sense- to begin to combine academic studies (say business) when a level of English at Intermediate / Upper Intermediate level has been achieved.

This mixture of English and academic studies may require advanced timetable planning and the Principal and DoS need to be aware of the class make up and throughput of all their students in order to ensure that students are not precluded from engaging on academic subjects by timetables that clash with their English lessons. One suggestion is to devote morning lessons to English and to plan the timetable for an introduction to professional subjects in the afternoon.

4.02 MEDIUM LENGTH COURSES

These are courses where tuition takes from 2 to 3 terms or semesters and is often restricted to certificates and diplomas in certain subjects. Normally the course is completed in 2 stages with assessment by examination between the first and second stage and a final examination or assessment at the end of the 3rd semester or 3rd term. Depending on the awarding body, the assessment can be either internally or externally set and assessed.

4.03 LONG COURSES

A long course can include First degrees and depending on the awarding, donor university, this degree may be awarded after 6 or 9 terms or semesters. The award of a first degree (BA [Hons], BSc. etc) by full time attendance at a UK university customarily lasts for 3 years, that is, 3 semesters or terms each of 10 / 12 weeks for each of 3 years. However depending on the donor university and the agreed method of teaching and assessment, some colleges negotiate variations from this and offer concentrated degree programmes. In these, completion can be in two academic years each of 3 semesters, where a semester lasts for 12 or 13 weeks. Another option is to offer 2 semesters of 18 weeks with college closure during the Christmas / New year and Easter holidays periods, as well as additional breaks for 'reading weeks' and revision prior to examinations. Details of semester and term provision are explained in the Introduction.

Longer semesters and less holiday can have the advantage to the student that a degree is completed in less time and although there may be little difference in the overall fee, the students' associated overheads are reduced by a large amount; student accommodation is only required for 2 years not three. The decision of the college about which structure to adopt is taken by the Academic Board, the Stakeholders and with guidance from the experience of the Principal. It can be more difficult to recruit teachers should the structure differ greatly from other local academic institutions.

With encouragement and if sufficiently motivated the student with a pass at 2.1 or above, can move on to acquire a higher, masters' degree earlier than in other organisations. A masters' degree can take as little as 3 terms or 3 semesters but the completion of a dissertation, an essential element of the award is made after success in the examinations at the end of the 3rd semester / term.

4.04 LEVEL – LOW / HIGH

Generally, low-level courses are those for which no formal qualifications are required for acceptance on the course. They can include the introductory levels of some professional courses (travel and tourism) or they can be the General Certificate of Secondary Education [GCSE] courses offered by many UK awarding bodies. They can also include Basic and Key skills, again offered by one of the 15 or so awarding bodies. An ability to read and write to an acceptable standard and to wish to progress is all that is required. These students are usually funded by one form of government organisation or another.

5] AWARDING BODIES & ACADEMIC PARTNERS

"Study the past if you would divine the future." Confucius (550 – 478 BCE)

Certificate level Decision about entry-level qualifications for commencing study; GCSEs, 'A' levels etc. English as a foreign language IELTS, ToEFL etc.

Diploma level Entry requirements and accreditation of prior knowledge;

Higher level Entry requirements and accreditation of prior knowledge; BSc / BA offering awards from a university partner then leading to MA MSc MBA offering awards from a university partner (not necessarily the same one)

Specialist subjects: a focus on a specialism, IT, languages, management, law, accountancy etc

5.00 ENGLISH LANGUAGE COURSES

The college can offer these for these reasons :

5.01 as a college income generator providing for those who want to learn English or improve their English for non-academic reasons. This can include non-English speaking immigrants who wish to achieve citizenship for which a knowledge of English language and English customs is required

5.02 To provide support and development for those students without the language abilities to begin a professional (Certificate / Diploma / Degree) programme.

5.03 As part of a 1 term **Academic Foundation Programme** of Study Skills; in this students spend 3 –5 hours / week developing their critical faculties covering the following: Report writing; essay planning; note-taking; oral presentation; skim reading; grammar; a typical Academic Foundation / Study Skills programme is shown in **Appendix 6.**

Students entering professional courses for Degrees etc. must be able to show proof of competence in English language and therefore an independent awarding body can provide assessment material. There are several such awarding bodies but the most usual are Pitman's, ToEFL (Test of English as a Foreign Language) and Cambridge University.

ToEFL offers one test, the grading of which indicates the student's ability; Cambridge and Pitman's offer tests at various levels from Foundation to Advanced.

Appendix 9 shows details of levels and description. A minimum of 60 hours tuition should be allowed for students' progress from one level to the next.

5.04 ENGLISH LANGUAGE COURSE DETAILS

All general English language courses include intensive grammar review and drills, reading practice with textual analysis, listening and speaking with conversation practice and pronunciation, vocabulary exercises, writing, using style and idioms, role playing and practical use of the language. Examination practice should be included at each level and internal evaluation should be on a continuous basis.

Course Length From 3 to 48 weeks. 4-6 weeks (60-100 hours) should be allowed for progress from one level to the next.

Dates Courses can start all year round. Each course can also be booked by the week, or several courses can be booked consecutively.

Course levels All levels, from elementary to advanced, can be offered. Students with previous knowledge of English take a placement test prior to the start of the course to ensure teaching is given at the appropriate course level and individual tuition should also be available.

Textbooks These are purchased by students and are not included in the course fees

5.05 CERTIFICATE AND DIPLOMA COURSES

Several awarding organisations listed in the Appendix [OCR – Oxford, Cambridge and RSA Examining Board; City & Guilds] offer certificates and diplomas in a wide range of subjects and the college may decide to offer many or some of them. It is advisable to restrict the number of organsiations that have to be dealt with and to reduce the subjects offered to a specific range, for example Business or Travel and Tourism. These restrictions make the administration of communication between awarding bodies, the college and the students more manageable. In addition, it is uneconomic to offer a wide range of subjects from several awarding bodies because classes take place with only a few students in each.

Whichever awarding body is selected, the award must be accredited by the Qualifications and Curriculum Development Agency [QCDA] whose approval indicates that the course on offer has academic merit and is assessed with rigour. It ensures students that the qualification is worth the paper it is written on.

Although qualifications in their own right, diploma courses are often a pathway to higher, university based qualifications such as first degrees and masters'. For example, the following Business Management programme is a professional, QCDA-accredited qualification to prepare students for a career in business, or to give advanced entry onto professional qualifications and university degrees in the UK and other countries.

The programme covers the theoretical issues of business and management and offers many practical skills useful to potential employers.

A typical business management **Curriculum** from certificate to Advanced Diploma is shown :

Certificate

- Introduction to Business
- Introduction to Quantitative Methods
- Introduction to Accounting
- Introduction to Business Communication

Diploma Part 1

- Economic Principles and their Application to Business
- Organisational Behaviour
- Financial Accounting
- Quantitative Methods for Business and Management

Diploma Part 2

- Marketing Policy, Planning and Communication
- Human Resource Management
- Management in Action
- Managerial Accounting
- Principles of Business Law
- Systems Analysis and Design
- Concepts and Principles of Islamic Economics

Advanced Diploma

- Corporate Strategy and Planning
- Managing in Organisations
- International Business Case Study
- Strategic Marketing Management
- Corporate Finance
- Strategic Human Resource Management for Business Organisation
- Managing the Information Resource
- Islamic Finance

5.06 BA (HONS) / BSC

Typically, these courses are offered in conjunction with a donor or partner university, which is usually responsible for the structure, curriculum and syllabus of the degree being taught by the college. A typical honours degree is in the UK offered over a 3 year period and is assessed by a combination of course work, examination and often, a dissertation.

A typical progression route as exemplified by the curriculum of the following Business Management degree shows:

YEAR 1

1. Organisations and Behaviour
2. Organisations, Competition and Environment
3. Marketing
4. Managing Financial Resources
5. Legal and Regulatory Framework
6. Management Information Systems
7. Quantitative Techniques for Business
8. Business Strategy

YEAR 2

9. Management Accounting
10. Managing Activities
11. Managing Self
12. Managing People
13. Managing Information
14. Human Resource Management
15. Marketing Planning
16. Quality Management

Some colleges, which offer the degree with a donor or partner university, use the following procedure. Upon successful completion of the first ten modules, students are awarded a BTEC Higher National Certificate while upon completion of all sixteen modules students will be awarded the BTEC Higher National Diploma, which will allow them direct entry to the final year of the BA (Hons) Business Management of the donor university. The students do have the option of transferring to other UK universities at this point if they wish to do so.

YEAR 3 - BA (Hons) Business Management top up

1. Financial Management
2. Strategic Management
3. Strategic Management of Human Resources
4. Contemporary Development in Management
5. Marketing Strategy
6. Managing Projects

On completion of a first degree, students are entitled to progress onto a Masters' programme. Again, this will be carefully supervised by the donor university who will supply teaching programmes, and curriculum and syllabus content. Depending on the arrangement between the partner university and the college, coursework and examinations may be set and marked by either. The exam grades and dissertation will be scrutinised and moderated thoroughly before the award of the higher degree.

A typical curriculum for a Masters' Degree in Management would contain the following.

Structure of the programme
Programme members complete six 20-credit module curriculum and a 60-credit project (a dissertation) as follows:

Strategic Planning and Policy Formulation (20 Credits)

Managing Information (20 Credits)

Managing People (20 Credits)

Managing Finance (20 Credits)

Managing Markets (20 Credits)

Research Methodology and Dissertation Planning (20 Credits)

the MSc Research Project (60 Credits)

Assessment
All 20 credit modules, except for the Research Methodology and Dissertation Planning module will typically require a coursework assignment of approximately 3,000 words which will contribute 50% of the total marks for the module, and a two-hour written examination or case study which contributes a further 50% of the module mark. However, depending on the university, other methods of assessment strategy may be used. The Research Methodology and Dissertation Planning module requires a detailed dissertation proposal. The Project module requires a submission of a research dissertation of between 10,000 and 15,000 words. The college will appoint a supervisor to guide each student through to completion of the dissertation.

Graduation
To be eligible for graduation and for the award of MSc Business Management course, members must gain 180 credits. Course members are normally required to obtain a minimum of 50 per cent in each module in order to qualify for the award of Master of Science (Pass). An MSc with Distinction may be awarded where a course member's average mark across the modules is 70 per cent or more.

ACCOMMODATING PART TIME STUDENTS

All the above courses are designed for **full time students** [FT] and the definition of a full time course is a course delivery to the students of at least 15 hours each week of the semester or term.

The college may wish to consider offering qualifications to **part-time students**, [PT] where student attend for 1 day a week or for 2 evenings each week or at week-ends.

Most host-universities and awarding bodies will accept this option because fees are still received and although the length of the course is extended, part-time students who often are in employment, are statistically more likely to have sufficient dedication and application complete their award.

The design of their attendance presents the college with choices; the DoS (or whoever compiles the timetables and appoints the teachers) has to decide whether or not the part-time students are to be accommodated within the existing course delivery programme. If this were achievable, there would be no impact on the engagement of teachers or on classroom allocation. On the other hand, when separate provision is made for part-time students, extra teachers have to be engaged and additional classrooms made available.

If these extra classes are offered outside normal teaching hours (09.00 – 18.00h Monday to Friday) it may be necessary to pay a higher hourly rate to teachers and the cleaning staff and the costs of servicing the college (electricity, heating etc) will increase. If the courses are offered at week-ends the costs will be considerably increased. The amalgamation of part-time students with full-time students can also present difficulties because FT students will progress more quickly; this can provide problems in group bonding. It is to be expected that the FT students will progress more rapidly than the PT students and so working together may be difficult. However, those in work can often bring life skills and practical examples when case studies or role-plays are part of the learning process.

As well as academic partners and a choice of awarding bodies, the college may wish to align itself with other **professional bodies**. These can provide guidance, an interchange of knowledge and connections with similar colleges. They also add credibility and breadth to the college's repertoire. Among many, one is **ECBE** (European Council for Business Education). It has a singular objective: supporting and sustaining the most rigorous quality of business education to achieve excellence in Business Education. ECBE claims that :

"to translate ***Excellence in Business Education*** *into reality for students' future careers, we are most keenly aware of the vital importance of the critical aspects of today's ever more competitive world. In turn, only Excellence in Business Education – and nothing less - will provide a rock solid foundation for the achievement of these* goals."

It states that its purpose and intent is to continually strive and to support excellence in superlative business education, by actively encouraging experimentation and profoundly superior levels of teaching. In addition it provide an interactive Forum which meets the educational challenges of relationships between governments, business, industry and academia and hosts an annual meeting at which representatives from dozens of European business colleges meet and participate in an exchange of ideas and methodology. ECBE demands, through its accreditation programme, that member institutions meet the requirements following the changes and developments recommended by the European Commission.

6] STAFF

"People who feel good about themselves produce good results". Blanchard & Johnson (The One Minute Manager1983)

We are going to examine all of the functions to be carried out within the college.

The **Organisation Chart** shown is for a college with 1,000 + students. With fewer students or with less variation in tuition offered, some of the functions may be combined.

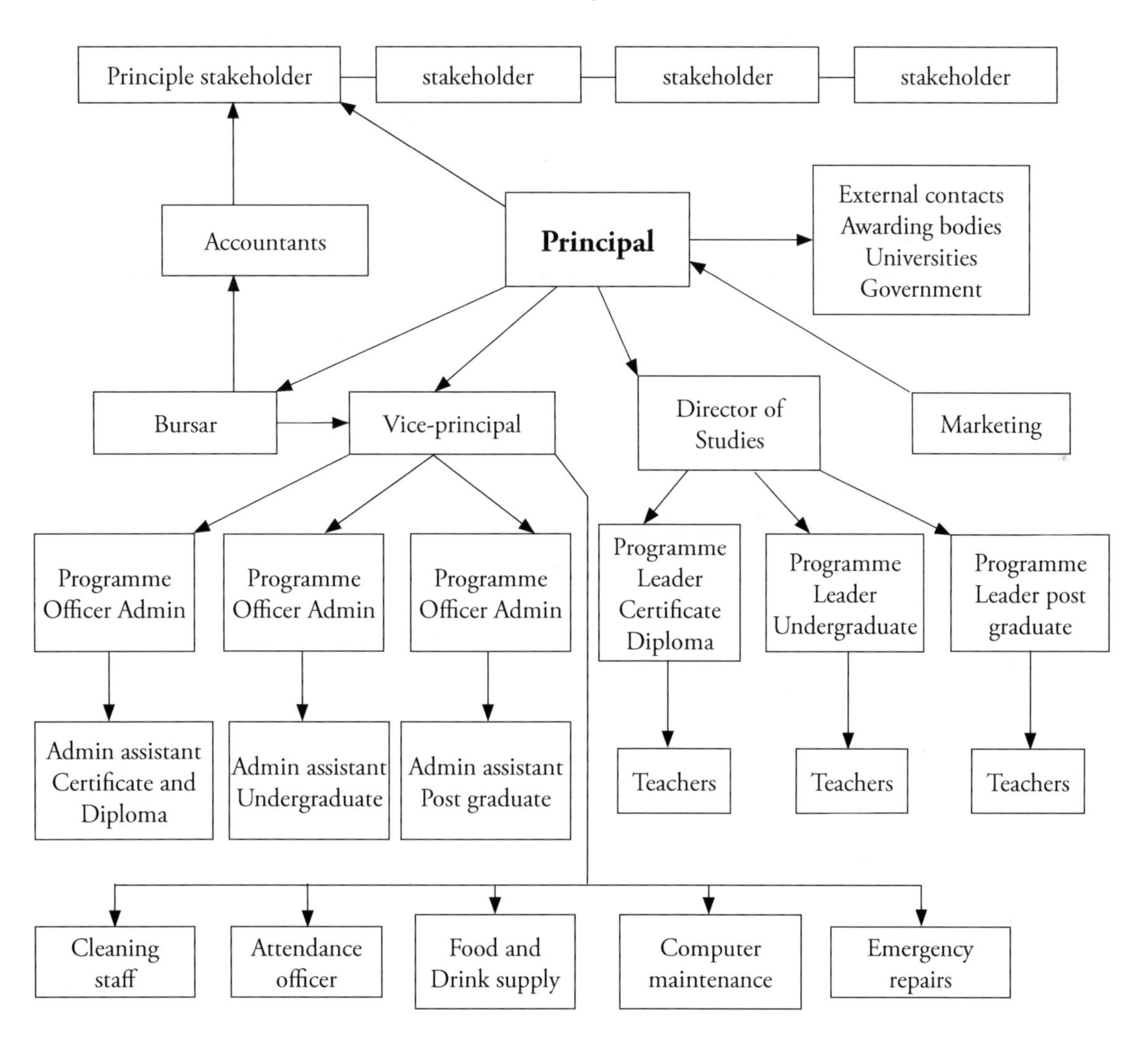

The personnel examined will include the following:

Stakeholders

Administrative staff: sufficient in number to provide for the student numbers and their requirements; **Bursar** (to collect fees in) and / or **Accountant** to pay out fees, taxes, invoices and wages; **Principal** (figurehead of the organisation); **Vice Principal** (VP); **Director of Studies** (DoS) to maintain standards, adherence to appropriate teaching methodologies, course programmes, curricula etc; **academic administrative staff** and **course** administrator(s) one for each programme and or each awarding body. **Accommodation officer**

Freelance / contract teachers: contract duration – by semester, term, course, and year. Payment per hour, per class, per term etc clear contract terms and conditions. Clear distinction between teacher responsibilities for absences – make-up classes or substitute teacher?

Cleaning staff, handymen,

Marketing staff / agents

Obviously, the number of staff depends on the size of college, number of courses offered and the number of students; in cases where the student numbers are low and / or the variety of courses is limited, some of the following roles will be combined BUT the functions to be carried out remain!

A detailed analysis of each function follows :

6.01 STAKEHOLDERS

These are the owners of the college; they may be shareholders, academics, directors or partners but their responsibility is to appoint staff to complete the mission statement of their enterprise. The **mission statement** is exactly that: a statement, which in a few words describes the reason for the existence of the college. For example, a mission statement can be:

"offering effective learning at effective prices."

or

"Our aim is to develop the individual within a social context of preparation for a future of unknown possibilities."

The college's mission statement will feature as prominently as its logo. (See **1.04**)

6.02 PRINCIPAL

The principal is the figurehead of the institution; although not necessarily a shareholder, he is responsible for directing the college in all its aspects. It is expected that he will identify what the college can do well, what organisations to link with, what success rate students should attain, what teachers are appointed and how they deliver their lessons; the principal is also responsible for ensuring that inspections by interested parties are successful; that visits from important organisations are conducted efficiently; that awarding bodies are welcomed and that everything possible is on hand as and when required. He should be available to provide wisdom and guidance to resolve internal and external conflicts; he is expected to be highly qualified and experienced; he is a manager not only a theorist. His practical talents should enable him in the absence of any of his staff to teach, to administer, and to access financial information.

He attends trade fairs and conferences and promotes his college at all times. He reports to the owners / stakeholders regularly addressing their requirements [especially financial] and makes recommendations as appropriate.

The Principal is ultimately responsible for all actions undertaken within the college and listed below, with observations, is the list of documentation identified in **2.18**

Company Accounts

The Bursar will maintain a copy of the last three years' accounts for inspection when legally required. The Principal will fully comprehend the balance sheet, the profit and loss account and will, in conjunction with accountants and stakeholders, prepare an analysis of *risk*. This involves preparation of calculations which detail the financial exposure of the college if future events happen (increase in student numbers), do not happening (failure of a marketing plan), if there are changes in expenditure (increase in local taxes) and changes in regulations.

Premises and Health and safety

Floor Plans of the College; these, produced by architects or surveyors and drawn to scale (1:100 or 1: 50) are useful to identify where facilities are located and to plan internal modifications to classrooms, library etc.

Health and Safety documentation showing all compliances. There are many of these. All relevant documentation must be located where it can be obtained at any time. A staff member is made responsible for all aspects of Health and Safety.

Fire precaution provision and a fire risk assessment; *means of escape* diagrams are a legal requirement and must be on display in all areas. The location of fire fighting equipment is identified on them. Signs showing Means of Escape with white lettering on green must be placed in locations advised by the local authority Fire safety Officer.

Necessary *Planning, Building Regulations* and *Environmental Health* Approvals. Access to these will be necessary if a challenge to the suitability or legality of the function of the building is made in the future.

Records of fire alarm practice and evacuation drills. Although a designated administrative assistant arranges for these exercises to occur at regular intervals, a record of each one must be kept and reviewed. Total evacuation of the premises should take less than 2 minutes.

Management and Staff Resources

Diagram of staffing structure see diagram **page 37**.

List of names and designations of staff. The designation should match the job description and is usually changed only after an appraisal and with the employee's consent

CVs of management, academic and senior staff (and passport / visa evidence of their entitlement to remain in UK) If the visa needs annual renewal, there needs to be a reminder system in place so it is useful to include a check-list of key dates, monitored by a dedicated member of staff.

Staff appointment procedure and *sample advertisements.* The method for the recruitment of admin. and teaching staff must be clear and strictly followed to avoid accusations of favouritism, bias or lack of equal opportunities.

Staff contracts These should be produced by a solicitor and should clearly identify :

a] hours to be worked b] rate of pay c] holiday entitlement d] disciplinary methods e] promotion / staff development opportunities f] period of appraisal review g] contract period if not open ended h] sickness policy i] time off in lieu (bereavement / family etc) j] initial trial period k] notice period.

Equal Opportunities policy. A clear and concise statement concerning ethnicity, sexual orientation, family responsibilities etc

Staff handbook. A volume containing all aspects of the way staff are managed and their obligations and entitlements. Additions and changes to the Staff Handbook should be clearly identified when a new edition is re-issued.

Procedures for *recording student attendance*, monitoring and taking action. The arrangements for signing in and the compilation of registers is explained in **6.04.02** but a staff member must be appointed to follow up the information to firstly identify students who are not attending for 80% of the time and then to put into action the sequence of phone calls, e-mails and letters shown in **6.07.01**

Procedures for examinations. Clearly written down and the responsibility of the VP

Procedures for the production of examination papers. A clear brief, identifying the relationship to what is in the syllabus and how and what is to be assessed with further details of arrangements for students with special needs. Assessment methodology is explored in **6.07.06**

Arrangements for the secure storage of examination papers and examination scripts. In a secure, lockable safe, often located in the office of the VP.

Minutes of Staff meetings and academic boards. Minutes are taken by an admin. member who files the signed minutes along with agenda. This function is described on the admin. member's job description and detailed in the staff handbook. The identification of various meetings is shown in **6.10**.

Evidence that staff qualifications have been verified. Once verified, the photocopied originals are signed and dated by the VP.

Teaching and Learning

Student application form. Usually a print out from the web site.

Pre-enrolment information for students dealing with course entry requirements, fees payable, documents required etc. Obtained from the web site and thorough. There must be no hidden surprises for the student.

Student handbook. Often presented on the web site but a clear document handed to and signed for by the student upon receipt. All aspects of life at the college are explained with thorough explanations of the implications of irregular attendance.

Course timetables showing minimum 15 contact hours / week for each course. Coffee breaks and refreshment periods are not to be included in class contact hours so a 3 hour lesson with a 15 minute break last 3 hours and 15 minutes and must be time-tabled as such.

Course descriptions, Course curricula, syllabi, course programmes These are detailed in the **Introduction.**

Learning outcomes, aims and objectives. The DoS monitors these from the teachers' lesson plans.

Samples of marked student work. Archive storage is required within the college for storing all students' work for 2 years then storing sample material for a further 5. This enables control and checks to be maintained on achievement year on year.

Emergency lesson plans held by the DoS (**see 6.04.01**)

Balanced work-load for students. This is the rationale for students whose studies include additional electives such as English language etc.

Sample examination papers. Archive storage will retain past exam papers from which samples can be obtained by 'cut and paste'.

Quality Control

Quality handbook / manual. This document identifies the postholder responsible for carrying out all of the functions of recording, maintaining and checking all aspects of management as well as suggesting alternative postholders to carry out the tasks in case of absence.

Records of meetings relating to curriculum development, course design, course review. An admin. staff member will be responsible for taking notes, writing up minutes and, after signing at the subsequent meeting, placing in archive storage.

Course approval documentation (for internally designed courses) written evidence of discussion and guidance.

Documentation confirming the level of courses internally designed and offered. Evidence that assessment criteria are in place to ensure students are tested at the appropriate level in an appropriate manner.

Records of student assessment (formal / informal; actual, predictive etc. The formal marked assessments, examination results and the marks for coursework, tests and internal and informal observations are kept in each student file and also in class files.

Student course evaluation forms. These are pre-printed forms filled in by each student during each course of their programme. Each course is evaluated anonymously on points such as subject delivery, depth of knowledge exposed, reading lists etc. The forms are returned and analysed and their contents summarised and the information presented to the Principal and the information made available to all teachers.

Records of meetings involving students. Minutes taken by an admin. member.

Procedure for selection of student representatives. A written policy included in the student handbook explaining the procedure for the election of one student member from each stage of each course.

Staff development policy and Staff appraisal records. Details of potential development are included in the staff contracts; appraisals prepare staff members for additional responsibilities and development. The college should recognise that its staff are its greatest resource (**see 6.09**)

*Teacher monitoring forms***.** The teachers' contracts identify that teacher monitoring will take place regularly. Advance notice of a monitoring visit by the DoS will be given. The information will be collected on the monitoring form (see **appendix 10**) and stored in the archives after analysis by the DoS.

Staff warning letters. The Principal's committee will agree on a procedure for advising teachers about disciplinary problems (persistent lateness, inappropriate behaviour with students etc.) and a series of warnings will be employed. There is no pro-forma letter but the sequence will be 2 verbal and two written. The VP initialises a similar procure for dealing with admin. staff.

Job Descriptions. A written description of the duties and functions involved in the post that the admin./ teacher fills.

Person Specifications. The qualities, experience and qualifications that the potential post holder must possess to be able to fulfil the job description.

Student Welfare

Pre-arrival information for International students about life in UK. A full explanation printed from the web site.

Meet and greet service and costs. A full explanation printed from the web site.

Accommodation service. A full explanation printed from the web site. If the college provides addresses for homestay accommodation, these locations must have been inspected and must meet minimum standards of space, hygiene and comfort.

Awards and Qualifications

Details of each course offered. This will be taken from the website and based on curricula offered either by the awarding body, the university partner or by an internally designed and approved course.

Guidance on academic misconduct. Included in the Student handbook; a list of unacceptable behaviour and the remedies the college will apply.

Evidence of formal arrangements and procedures in place with awarding bodies, university partners etc. Signed originals and photocopies of the contract setting out all terms and conditions and timescales (duration of the arrangements, grounds for cancellation etc.)

Examination boards - minutes, mark sheets etc. Copies of appropriate mark sheets, observations, and marked sample scripts.

Marketing and Student recruitment

Ethics policy. A clear and concise statement explaining the attitude of the college and its employees towards students about ethnicity, sexual orientation, family responsibilities etc.

Criteria for the appointment of agents. How they are selected, how their legality is checked and how and when they are paid for what they do.

Agency agreement. An actual and sample contract.

Briefing document for agents.

Prospectus. A print out from the website; professionally designed and printed in full colour on quality paper (100g / m2)

Procedures for processing enquiries and applications. Clear identification of individual and back up post holders' responsibilities to analyse enquiries and applications (on line and postal); check applicants' qualifications, and present lists to the Admissions Committee.

Procedures relating to student admission and enrolment. From list of accepted students, copies of sample e-mail and postal letters which are sent to students. Confirmation of visa entry requirements and start dates for course on which student has been accepted. (see **3.01**)

Procedures for monitoring students' academic progress. Marks awarded to all students - for exams, tests, and coursework are passed to the college IT section to be centrally entered onto the college data base. Weekly, all class / course marks are interrogated by a designated admin. member and, working to previously agreed guidelines, a list of students whose marks cause concern is handed to the VP.

Procedures for handling deposits, fee payments and refunds. A copy of the written policy is included in the quality manual and the Bursar works to these criteria. (see **3.01.11**)

Press cuttings. The marketing section should initiate favourable press cuttings and retain and utilise such publicity effectively. (see **chapter 8.00**)

6.03 VICE-PRINCIPAL (VP)

Deputy to the principal in name but charged with a separate set of responsibilities and functions, the VP carries out the administrative functions devolved from the Principal; the VP substitutes for the Principal when absent but also carries out many of the functions required of the principal; he organises and checks the bursar's income and expenditure statements and (often) signs the cheques for payment. Frequently the expenditure of items of capital equipment is devolved to him so he is expected to make an analysis before making decisions on what items to purchase; he attends most internal meetings with the Principal but chairs others.

Often the VP is responsible for the examinations carried out in the college; some colleges act as 'centres' for examinations taken by external students - either self-taught or from other local colleges. The VP has to receive the examination papers, keep them secure until the day of the examination, and after the examination collect them back in along with the students' scripts. He assumes responsibility for sending everything back to the examining body promptly. For this, a secure safe is required with appropriate safeguards.

The VP is also responsible for all aspects of health and Safety [H&S] throughout the college; he has to maintain the safety of electrical equipment, arrange for certificates of safety for all portable appliances, of computer facilities, including updating programs to ensure freedom from virus attack and hacking. His most important role in H&S is to regularly carry out fire drills through testing the means of escape procedures. Once a week the fire alarms should be sounded and at frequent but not regular intervals, full evacuation of the building should take place. All such details are to be recorded and the information collated and stored. Such records form part of many of the inspection procedures of governmental inspecting bodies. (See **2.18)**

Another role often delegated to the VP and his admin.staff, is the methodology of allocating student **Identification Numbers (IDs**). IT access is required for rapid information about individual students and it must be easy to interrogate computer programs to obtain such information. ID numbers, as well as applying to individual students, should also contain - within the number itself - information about the student and / or course. Some colleges identify each student by their initials and date of birth. For example, student George Anthony Patel, born on 23 April 1990 would be identified as ID GAP230490.

Another form of ID number could comprise the enrolment date and course; Mr Patel would be given the ID 2009BAHons / 01 indicating that he was the first student in 2009 to enrol on the Honours degree course. Subsequent students would be numbered 02, 03 etc.

There should be a **Director of Studies** [DoS] with higher qualifications and greater experience.

6.04 DIRECTOR OF STUDIES [DOS]

6.04.01 What does the DoS do? What experience is needed? Well, he is the 'team captain' the liaison between principal and teaching staff and one who ensures the delivery of what is needed [the course] to those who need it [the students] all in accordance with the mission statement. He has the responsibility to verify the work of the teachers and provide evidence of their teaching ability and classroom management by formal monitoring of their work. A monitoring form is shown in **Appendix 10.**

Often the DoS plans the timetable; this allows him to link the interaction between, for example English language, academic subjects with similar and / or progressive courses; it helps ensure that teachers achieve the most effective delivery of their course and the most effective use of their (expensive) time; he ensures that students do not spend long periods of inactivity waiting between classes and he can also minimise the teaching of classes late into the evening when the mental faculties of both teachers and students are often diminished. He allocates the most appropriately laid-out classroom for each teacher's specific purpose, some with a formal layout others without.

The DoS has overall sight of the content (via the lesson plan) of each class and is aware of how each class is part of the overall syllabus and how each syllabus is part of the overall curriculum. This should allow him to ensure that classes, where different teachers are teaching similar core themes but in different course programmes, are able to present them in a similar way with minimum time between such imput. This allows the learners to receive a clear-cut definition of the subject, which can be reinforced when taught in a subsequent class on a different course.

The experience needed for this role then requires, apart from obvious HRM skills, knowledge of the components of the separate courses comprising the overall syllabus together with their learning outcomes and how they are to be assessed. Knowledge of the progression from one course to another is needed. To be in this position requires extensive study of the material issued by the awarding bodies but this also benefits the DoS in the appointment of the teachers chosen to deliver the separate elements and subjects of the course.

In conjunction with the wishes of the Principal, the DoS implements policy when teachers are unavailable through illness or absence. Either this is for the lesson to be cancelled and made up at a later date or for another member of staff to take the class. If the former, it requires fitting in another lesson at a later date which may be at an inconvenient time. In addition, students who cannot be forewarned, are upset if they have made a long and expensive journey only to find the lesson is not taking place. A more satisfactory solution, when students cannot be forewarned is for a lesson to take place with another teacher or with the DoS. The DoS will have collected from each teacher an **'emergency lesson'** which is described on a lesson plan and which the DoS or another can implement. It will not introduce much new material but will be a lesson plan designed to emphasis previous knowledge and contextualise it more thoroughly; it will be a student led lesson, something the students often enjoy. For these reasons, the DoS should be a qualified teacher.

6.04.02 STUDENT ATTENDANCE. The DoS is normally responsible for organising the collection of attendance data; normally, registers form the raw data for compiling attendance records. The register is completed either once or twice during each lesson by the lesson's teacher. One successful way is to ask the students to fill in an attendance sheet on which they record their name, **ID number** (see **6.03**) and signature. This attendance sheet is then collected in and a line drawn beneath the last signature 20 minutes after the lesson begins. The teachers' role is detailed further in **6.07**. A second attendance sheet is provided after any coffee break during the lesson.

6.05 BURSAR It is the bursar who takes on responsibility for the receipt and expenditure of monies associated with the running of the college. He must programme how much is expected to be collected from student application fees, course tuition fees, both private and government funded and provide a balance between income and projected expenditure such as rent / mortgage, council tax, salaries, books, computers, utilities etc. He should forecast each of these and provide continuous updates of how actual income is matching the anticipated income, how expenditure is matching anticipated costs and must be able to provide evidence of how accurately costs were projected.

Regularly, the bursar writes the cheques for all payments especially salaries and arranges transfer of funds within the bank to meet the payments due.

When required the bursar liases with the **accountant;** the accountant at appropriate times produces a balance sheet and profit and loss account and these are presented to the stakeholders and submitted to government financial / company organisations when legally demanded.

6.06 COURSE DIRECTOR(S) This function is also known as **programme manager** or **module leader**. There should be one course director for each separate academic programme for example one Course Director for the BA (Hons) 3 year programme; another for the 1 year ABE Certificate in Business Studies etc.; he should be aware of the component elements of the course (the subject modules which constitute the course) and is expected to be aware of the structure, syllabus, inter-relationship and lesson plans, assessment methodology and future pathways of all aspects of his course. He often teaches one or more of the subjects on the course and acquires knowledge of the students on it; he also acts as an advisor to individual students on all aspects of their studies and / or personal life. He also works with the teachers in the design of the course programmes and often sits on the admissions' panel.

Larger colleges often delegate a staff member as 'attendance officer'.

6.07 TEACHERS:

Salaried or free-lance status

Many colleges are unable to offer full-time teaching posts to many of their teaching staff; a college is not a school and unless the student cohort is very large it is uneconomic to employ salaried teachers whose teaching hours will be less than a full week. Many teachers are therefore designated **part-time but salaried**, where the college deducts income tax and national Insurance and pays them when ill, or **self-employed** and paid on invoices for the hours actually taught with no deductions for tax and national Insurance. However, the Inland Revenue [IR] may require that invoices for teacher hours are made through a registered **partnership, sole trader** or limited liability **company**. The college will be charged with paying any income tax not deducted from teacher payments if the IR does not consider the teacher to be genuinely self - employed. Under the definitions above, teachers must be able to show that other employment is carried out in other locations and / or another teacher from the partnership / company could fulfil the role at the college if required.

It is important that the status of all staff is clearly defined with a contract and letter of appointment in which the terms and conditions are clearly stated. It should be made clear what action is to be taken about illness, inability to teach, holidays etc. Remember financially, the college is responsible for remedying any underpaid tax if the Inland Revenue disagrees about the status of college teachers who have been paid as self-employed.

The contract should also confirm what other duties are to be performed (exam supervision, exam setting, marking, counselling etc) and what rate of pay, if any, is attracted by these duties.

The frequency of appraisals or monitoring visits should be stated together with the availability of pay enhancement for extra classes or extra responsibilities and the opportunities for internal promotion (to course director or other positions)

The opportunity to obtain further qualifications, time off for courses, Continuing Professional Development [CPD] etc. must all be provided in writing, not just to preclude any future disputes but to adhere to the requirements of ASIC or IiP or other organisations whose recognition may be sought by the college

Teachers are encouraged to negotiate with the students what is to be done with late arriving students; late arrivals can disrupt the lesson and it is usually agreed that students who arrive 20 minutes or more after the beginning of the class will not be allowed entry nor disturb the lesson. They are to return to the class and sign the attendance sheet after the break. **See 6.04.02.**

The teacher later enters attendances onto the official register. Colleges often take the register twice, before and after a break. Attendance records are then entered into the college data base and examined weekly to determine the level of absences. This allows the college to determine students who are habitually late for classes or who do not attend for the whole length of the lesson. Frequent absences are reported by the DoS to the Government as infrequent attendees are considered not to be genuine students and can have their student status withdrawn as follows:

6.07.01 As stated in the **student terms and conditions** warning letters for non-attendance will be sent as follows:

- 1st letter – after one week's unexplained absence
- 2nd letter – after 2 weeks absence and no response
- 3rd letter – after 3 weeks absence, no response and terminating the registration of the student and with a letter to the Home Office.

6.07.02 LEGAL CLEARANCE

If the college seeks approval from the British Council or from ASIC where students between the ages of 16-19 are enrolled it may be necessary to ensure that all staff who have contact with these students have been cleared by the Criminal Records Bureau (CRB) Some young students either local or from outside the UK are considered to be 'vulnerable' adults. Those college employees who have the care and concern as part of their responsibilities, need to have clearance that they have no outstanding criminal record that might be considered relevant to the safety and well-being of the students. Further information is available on www.crb.gov.uk

6.07.03 QUALIFICATIONS.

All appointed teachers should possess appropriate qualifications and experience; for professional subjects, a qualification in the appropriate discipline (RICS, CIM, ACCA, etc) is essential and a teaching qualification (PGCE, Cert.Ed. City &Guilds 7407 etc) is very desirable. Those without a teaching qualification should begin a formal course and / or take part in a short intensive 20 / 30 hour course. These teacher-training programmes enable the students to receive teaching at the high level and with the expertise that such training provides. The college should, as a minimum, introduce its unqualified staff to a short intensive internal teacher-training programme - even a course of one or two days has immense benefits.

Students leave colleges for many reasons but bad and ineffective teaching is the most common reason.

English language teachers should have CELTA, [Certificate in English Language Teaching to Adults] or the DELTA [the higher, Diploma qualification] awarded by Trinity College or Cambridge University showing that the teachers have acquired a level of proficiency in teaching English as a foreign language to adults. The advantages to all teachers, not just of English language but also of business subjects having these CELTA qualifications are immense. The knowledge of the grammar of language helps teachers identify the problems some students experience in studying in a language other than their mother tongue. Such knowledge helps teachers structure their vocabulary and explanations in a way that students find easier to understand.

Previous experience in teaching is also desirable. Voluntary teaching or delivery of work-based or in-house training offers experience and adds confidence in delivering lessons.

Teachers should be aware of their responsibilities to plan their classes with precision so that fee - paying students receive full benefit for their choice of learning.

A conference in early 2000 suggested that:

"teaching is a complex, multi-faceted art and the role of teachers is changing from being not just navigators of learning but to becoming professionals who have skills in identifying the place, pace, time and methodology of learning most suited to each learner." Twining (2000)

6.07.04 TEACHING DOCUMENTATION

The Director of Studies may want to ensure that all teaching staff are advised what is expected of them. There are key documents that need to be produced and understood by all teachers. These are:

Course Curriculum
Syllabus
Course Programme
Lesson Plan

The **Course Curriculum** as explained in the Introduction and identified in 5.06.01 is a document listing all the subjects and modules to be taken over the full length of the course (for example 3 years for a First degree or 1 year for a Certificate in Business) In the case of an awarding body or partner university, this material is produced by them.

The **Syllabus** is a document expanding in more detail the contents of each subject, or module, within the Course Curriculum. In the case of an awarding body or partner university, they often also produce this material. In 5.6.01 the syllabus would detail what is included in each of the 16 course modules in years 1 and 2 and in the 6 course modules in year 3.

The **Course Programme,** one for each module, is a document designed by the Director of Studies, with assistance from the Course Director. For example in the case of module 1 in 5.6.01 Organisation and Behaviour, the course programme lists lesson by lesson the key elements of the module which are to be tested at the end of the learning programme.

The DoS is perhaps the most appropriate staff member to compile the Course programme because he has an overall picture of the Course Curriculum and the Syllabus; in it, using knowledge and skill, the content, the aims and objectives of each lesson are chosen. This enables an inter-relationship between different course programmes or modules to be discussed so that a consistency in overall approach between related but separate modules can be chosen.

The Lesson Plan shown in **Appendix 7** is a document produced by the teacher of each separate module and shows how what has been decided in the course programme is delivered to the students. The teachers provide a copy of all lesson plans to the DoS.

Again, in module 1 Organisation and Behaviour the teacher would provide a series of lesson plans which show what is to be taught in each lesson, how it is to be delivered, the resources needed and how the knowledge delivered is to be assessed at the lesson's end.

There is no reason why the teachers cannot also fulfill the roles of Programme Manager or Module Director and in fact, this is often the case.

The Director of Studies may wish to offer guidance to the teaching staff in the way that their work is performed. He may advise that what is done in the classroom must be meticulously planned.

The DoS may advise that teachers that:

"Your activities there must be as rehearsed as those of an actor. Why? Because you have limited time with the learners - limited contact hours in which you have the opportunity to inspire, lead, guide and thrill them, limited time to provide them with the skills they will take with them for the rest of their lives not just knowledge with which to pass examinations. Therefore, every moment must be planned to ensure that you do not waste their precious and expensive time. You must be certain you know exactly what you have to teach, when it should be taught to obtain best advantage; you should know how your particular subject relates to the overall course being taken. All this must be planned.

Planning involves preparation of the materials you will use, memory aids for the sequencing of its delivery and details of how it and in what 'language' it is to be presented.

Some of the documents that you, the subject teacher will be involved with in the planning of the lesson are:

Course curriculum: ask yourself or find out

what is the overall course the students are following?

how many subjects does it contain?

what vocabulary is unique, possibly unknown, in a strange context and / or contains words where synonyms – words with the same meaning - are not easy to find?

does any other subject-matter over-lap with yours?

how do the separate parts inter-relate? For example, are other teachers delivering similar aspects of the same subject? If so, you should harmonise to ensure the contents are interpreted in a similar way and to ensure that important vocabulary is explained in the same way at least twice.

Are there similar or over-lapping parts that perhaps could be taught around the same time during the term? There are advantages to the learners if you and colleagues can design **course programmes** and teach complementary aspects of a subject during the same week."

Syllabus

As well as accepting advice from the DoS, each teacher should identify:

the percentage of the total course curriculum is his syllabus? Is it 20% or 5% of the students' total learning? What is the exact content of the subject he is responsible for? Does he have to make decisions about what is and is not included? Is he happy with the textbooks recommended? Are they up to date? Do they contain difficult vocabulary or obscure grammar that learners would find difficult?

Course programme:

This document shows what is to be taught- lesson by lesson- and during which lesson each aspect of the syllabus is to be covered.

Lesson plans

These contain the content of each lesson by which teachers deliver the course programme:

Lesson plans should identify one or 2 aims for each lesson and several objectives and the lesson plan should divide the lesson-time into sections of about 20 minutes to reflect the students' limited concentration span. Identify key words in the Aims and Objectives and repeat them frequently during the lesson.

6.07.05 INTER-RELATIONSHIPS

An explanation of each of the above follows which shows how they are inter-related.

Teachers rarely have control of the course curriculum; in order to acquire knowledge about a specific programme or qualification, learners are presented with documentation, which indicates the subjects to be studied normally over a specified period of time - a term, semester or year. This is the **curriculum** but teachers are also presented with a syllabus. This identifies the content within each separate subject within the curriculum for which they are responsible.

This **syllabus** identifies the content of all the learners' overall programme of study for one subject. Often an explanation is given of the relative importance - the 'weighting' - given to different parts of the syllabus. It lists the concepts, underpinning knowledge and facts that the learners are expected to understand, remember and interpret at the end of the period of study. It sometimes apportions weighting or suggests that some aspects are of more importance than others are and should be taught as such.

This syllabus information has to be interpreted onto a **course programme**: a lesson-by-lesson time-table of what is to be taught and when. This document will show, for each session of the course, the main topics and subsidiary topics that are to be covered, their relationships within the overall programme, references, dates of relevant assignments or tests and when revision or formal testing will occur. It is a document showing when each part of the syllabus to be taught Teachers may or may not contribute to its formation, as it is often a task completed by the Programme Manager or Module Leader in conjunction with the Director of Studies.

The task of the teacher- as the subject expert - is to analyse and portion up the course programme into lessons, covering, during the total lessons that are to be delivered, all of the relevant parts of the Course programme. The focuses shown in the course programme are overarching information that is fundamental to this part of the course; the course programme should be handed to students when classes first begin.

From this, teachers plan each lesson in the form of a **lesson plan**. This lesson plan is the document which identifies the aim [s] and objectives that the learners need to know at the end of the lesson; objectives are more specific and subsidiary than the aims and often answer the question '*...at the end of the lesson the learners will know....*(objective 1,2 etc)'. However, more importantly, the lesson plan shows HOW teachers facilitate the learning and in what ways the lesson is divided into discrete parts.

The **lesson plan** shows the following which should be included:

Course Title

The **number** of each lesson in the series making up the course programme

Aim[s] and Objectives

Interaction: who is communicating with whom; is it students working together in pairs or individual work or class/group discussion or a teacher led debate or a lecture?

Topic: exactly what you want students to have learnt during each discrete part of the lesson and how it is to be accomplished. Is it an idea, a new way of looking at facts and is it best learnt by demonstration, discovery learning, by listening, by seeing etc?

Timing: how long are you allowing for completing topics or the learning objectives in each part of the lesson?

Assessment: how will you measure that the learning objectives have been accomplished? This does not have to be a written test but a non-formal or, if you choose, formal series of questioning, oral or written or observation, to ensure that you have passed on the objectives at the top of your lesson plan and that the learners have understood the aims of the lesson.

Also on the lesson plan should be identification of your role at each part of the lesson - controller or participant or prompter or observer; you should also write in the plan when you propose to introduce music to act as an additional segmentation-aid to the break up the lesson into discrete parts to take advantage of the limited concentration span of the learners.

To achieve this you should:

recognise that after about 20 minutes students will require a change in teaching methodology in order to help them concentrate, learn and remember

announce just before changing the methodology that this change is going to happen; this has the effect of 'kick starting' the students' ability to absorb and concentrate [in anticipation of the 'new' methodology] and you or they should quickly summarise the contents of the previous 20-minute segment. If the learners summarize, it reinforces their learning. These 20 minutes and the methodologies incorporated within them are all to be written down on the lesson plan.

The lesson plan identifies the methodologies to be employed. You need to know some of the variety of methodologies available and at your disposal, their particular advantages and disadvantages and how and when they should be employed, always remembering that you are teaching the students, not the subject.

Teachers are also expected to fulfil other duties such as administration and student counselling and allowance in the paid hours should provide for this.

6.07.06 ASSESSMENT

Teachers and programme managers and course leaders, as well as the Director of Studies, should all be aware of the **assessment methods** employed by each of the awarding bodies for each of the courses offered. Some awarding bodies assess student entirely by an examination taken on prescribed dates; others allow teachers to assess some of the courses work and an examination carries a percentage of the overall mark.

The Assessment procedures should be made clear to all teaching staff and all students. They should be both rigorous and transparent.

There follow notes on assessment.

Different types of assessment

It depends on why we are assessing but generally we assess **formally** or **informally**, in writing, role play or orally, alone or in groups, as a whole class or individually

Formal assessment may take the form of a written test or some tangible and recordable form, (such as the adequate completion of a product or a video of student performance) which will demonstrate that learning has taken place. This is usually done on an individual basis at the end of a period of learning, often by examination.

Informal assessment usually takes place more frequently, (end of a lesson, every week etc) in the form of Q and A or brainstorm where students make suggestions showing mastery of what has been learnt; a self-marked mini test is another format. Such responses are not usually recorded.

HOW DOES ASSESSMENT TAKE PLACE?

By ensuring that the assessment vehicle meets the following criteria:

Reliability
Validity
Currency
Sufficiency
Differentiation
Cost / time effectiveness
Authenticity
Clear instructions
Subsidiary skills
Transparency
Fitness for purpose
Time constrained
Cultural and religious bias

RELIABILITY :

Would the same assessment in the same circumstances and with the same student cohort give the same results if marked by different markers? Would multiple choice questions, essay questions or oral exams produce the same result? *What would add to reliability? :*

- More than one marker of each script, marks averaged
- Clear written marking scheme with bullet points
- Restricted 'grades' available - pass /fail
- Short questions
- Consistent circumstances
- Do written free-answer (essay) tests make consistent marking more difficult?

VALIDITY

Does the vehicle actually test what it claims to test? (ESOL at BASIC level / FRENCH conversation etc) It should match the assessment to the teaching (if it wasn't taught, don't test it)

What would add to validity?

- Assessment based on learning goals/aims/objectives and teaching methods
- assess many objectives not just a few
- clear objectives and clear criteria (simple instructions)

CURRENCY:

Is the subject matter up to date; is the knowledge the students must demonstrate modern and best practice?

SUFFICIENCY

Are most of the learning aims and objectives being tested or only a few?

DIFFERENTIATION / discrimination :

Is there the opportunity for the well-read students to achieve considerably more in the assessment than the lazy student?

Do multiple-choice tests discriminate against the more able? Remember students learn (and forget) at different rates.

COST / TIME EFFECTIVENESS

Can a fair assessment be carried out within time limits that are not excessive to the students and the invigilator; must sufficiency be compromised by time? How are a large enough number of objectives tested?

Can the assessment be carried out without incurring a disproportionately high financial cost which (ultimately) is met by the student?

AUTHENTICITY: does the assessment test what is easy to test OR test what should be tested?

INTRUCTIONS / PRACTICE:

Have the students been told beforehand exactly how they will be assessed?

Are the instructions about what they have to do been clearly written down?

(Example: Consider that Level 1 ESOL – instructions on what to do and how to fill in the answer paper may sometimes be written at level 3!)

Allow students to practise on past papers / tests in a similar format.

SUBSIDIARY SKILLS:

If the students are being assessed in (say) chemistry, does it matter that they make grammatical mistakes in their English? If ESOL students write incorrect facts in perfect English, should they be penalised? In ESOL oral: should good pronunciation be more important than grammar?

TRANSPARENCY

Every aspect of preparing the students for assessment, participating in assessment and marking the assessment vehicle must stand up to rigorous scrutiny; every question, procedure, mark and comment must be able to be justified. This is especially relevant in internal college tests to determine students' ability to pass to another level.

Assessment often includes discrete elements: *attendance mark, contribution in class mark, coursework mark, and exam mark.* These must be accurately recorded, weighted (if so agreed) and substantiated with meticulous and objective record keeping. Any subjective marks must be justified very carefully!

FITNESS FOR PURPOSE

Whatever assessment methodology is chosen it must be the correct one for the students, teacher, institution, stakeholders etc. and be defensible!

TIME CONSTRAINED...?

Are you testing speedwriting or subject knowledge? Should a slow reader of questions (who nevertheless has other high abilities) be penalised? Can you be flexible to obtain a fair assessment?

CULTURAL AND RELIGIOUS BIAS

Are tests taken during fasting or late on at the end of a long day, useful in assessing abilities or memory?

Some cultures are more used to oral testing than written assessments. Do written tests penalise them?

OTHER COLLEGE STAFF

6.08 ANCILLARY STAFF

As well as managers, admin. staff and teachers, a college cannot function without other vital people.

Cleaning Staff: Students are often untidy and at the end of a college day, everything must be cleaned up ready for the next day. Toilets must be cleaned, classrooms emptied of papers and bottles, floors cleaned and forgotten books and personal effects returned to the VP. This is the opportunity to record things broken [door handles, light bulbs, fluorescent tubes] or missing [notices, signs, loo paper] and to pass such information onto whoever is responsible, often the VP. For things that require building work or professional skills (electrical or plumbing etc) the VP should have emergency access to a **handyman** or a similar trade organisation; college education cannot be delayed while waiting for builders to arrive and repair essentials.

The desks and chairs should be put back in place, the white boards chemically cleaned and the toilet and washing and kitchen facilities hygienically washed down.

6.09 STAFF MONITORING AND APPRAISAL

As good as the groups of college employees may be, the college has both obligations and the need for upholding good practice to ensure that their tasks are being fulfilled in the way the stakeholders demand and this is done by **Appraisal**

Good college management evaluates its entire staff, its teachers, admin. and others on a regular basis. The purpose of this Evaluation or Appraisal is to ensure that:

1. The work done is done in a way that is intended
2. The worker is adequately trained and experienced to do what is asked of him
3. Good practices are rewarded and bad practices eradicated

Appraisals should take place regularly so that the contribution of all members of the college team has the opportunity to respond to the 3 items above.

An appraisal is a formal conversation with a purpose between a manager and a staff member or DoS and teachers to discuss their performance over a fixed period of time, usually 3 or six months or a year (or since the previous appraisal) and can coincide with any annual salary review or a proposed change of status.

Appraisals benefit both the organisation and the individual in a variety of ways. Organisations that believe and properly invest in their staff training and development gain culturally and financially and appraisals play a key role in staff retention as it allows staff to be adequately trained and developed. The financial benefit occurs when staff are trained up to undertake roles that would often have to be filled by external recruitment.

Appraisals should also be seen as a symbol of investing in the future of the college rather than as a chore. Some organisations both like and dislike appraisals for many reasons. Primarily because they place subjective judgement onto a more objective basis, which can often be open to scrutiny. Then, instead of bringing staff and management closer together, it can do the opposite and alienate them from one another.

The best appraisals involve a great deal of preparation by the **appraiser** and the **appraisee**. Ideally, as much notice as possible should be given to allow for the collection of evidence such as examples of work, letters of thanks and results of courses attended. In the case of teachers, the exam successes of their students, their course evaluation results are all made available. In order for appraisals to be successful, they must be set up in a system that is simple, flexible and easy to operate within cultural or organisational norms to achieve results.

The main objective for organisations during appraisals is to ensure that the aims of both the organisation and the individual's are co-ordinated, that staff are clear about their responsibilities, that lines of communication are improved and that there are greater exchanges of ideas.

The main objective for managers (in the case of the admin. staff) and the VP or DoS (in the case of teachers) during appraisals is to determine whether the original job description is still valid or whether it has been overtaken by events, if the job is causing the subordinate any problems and if they are, how they might be resolved and if any additional help is required.

The main objective for an **appraisee** during appraisals is to see how well he is performing to meet targets over a defined period of time and how well he is coping in his role. Performance is measured realistically in quantifiable or objective (never qualitative or subjective) targets with specific time spans for achievement which is agreed by the both the appraiser and the appraisee.

During the interview, it is important to be in a neutral location that is quiet and free from interruption. Often appraisals take place in an adjacent café or meeting room or library so that the appraisee does not feel intimidated in the office of the appraiser.

A strong emphasis should also be placed on a two-way conversation rather than a one-sided interview. It is paramount that managers establish a good rapport and begin with the positive aspects of performance. The appraisee should be allowed time to answer any criticisms. The manager also needs to identify any training needs, timetable them and follow them through. The manager should lead the appraisee in analysing and solving his performance difficulties through a structured discussion incorporating good questioning techniques that allow the appraisee to enter into a discussion. Open or closed questions can be used but not leading or multiple questions as this can be both confusing and a pointless form of questioning.

The feedback is given to the appraisee later - after reflection - and should not overload him with too many negative points as this can be quite frustrating. The advice given should be clear, concise and constructive, in a manner that is understandable so that he can rectify problems, set targets and improve performance in general.

There are two types of appraisals:

Judgemental appraisals relate to current performance in a particular job, and it is often linked to pay (performance related pay) and

Development appraisals, which seek to identify and develop potential for future performance, linked to succession and personal development planning.

A typical **appraisal form** is included in **Appendix 8**

It is also the responsibility of the college to provide teacher monitoring and this although separate from appraisals serves to ensure that the teachers are competent and effective. A **teacher monitoring form** is included in **Appendix 10.**

6.10 COLLEGE DECISION MAKING

In order for the college to run effectively and for decisions made by the management to be received by the staff, various committees are recommended.

Meetings of these committees are held regularly at set intervals in order to consider all aspects of the running of the college. The VP usually plans the dates of such meetings and produces agendas and arranges for the publication of minutes. Some of these committees and their functions and chair are described below.

Academic Committee : once each term / semester all teaching staff meet with the Principal, VP and DoS to receive information about any changes in university partnerships, potential changes in awarding bodies or courses offered and future plans for increases or decreases in courses, programmes or students and financial details affecting the teaching staff. *Chair : Principal*

Student / Staff Liaison Committee : each student cohort is asked to elect a student representative to attend this committee's meeting each term / semester. Its purpose is to listen to, explain, justify or act on student complaints, questions or worries.

Chair : Vice Principal

College / Partnership Committee : regular meetings take place with each of the college partners, the universities or awarding bodies. Meetings with the universities are held for specific purposes, predominantly to agree standards in examination results and to assess coursework. Specific meetings take place at the end of term or semester to evaluate student performance and agree lists of students eligible to proceed to the next stage of a qualification. These meetings are usually chaired by the university / awarding body and the respective programme managers / module leaders are invited to comment on the performance of their student cohort. External verifiers who have examined a sample of the college students' work offer observations about the marks and marking. *Chair : Visiting University / Awarding Body*

Health and Safety [H&S] Committee : at regular intervals an examination is made of all aspects of H&S; means of escape and fire precautions are reviewed and the analysis of recent 'mock' fire alarm drills is reviewed. *Chair : Vice Principal.*

Planning and Resources Committee : Once or twice a year representatives of the stakeholders meet with the Principal, VP and DoS and Bursar to examine the aspects of cost and expenditure. The meeting analyses the current ratio of income to expenditure, the future demands of financial expenditure and the proposed future income from each of the sources identified in Chapter One. *Chair : Stakeholder.*

Admissions Board : when there are sufficient applicants for enrolment, the VP, DoS and senior academic staff meet to evaluate the applications. They consider the students' qualifications, life experience and work experience. Its purpose is to offer advice about each potential student, offering or declining the application, taking into account how potentially successful the applicant may turn out to be. *Chair : DoS.*

Heads of Department Meetings : at the beginning of each term / semester a meeting is held between the Programme Managers and the DoS, Its purpose is to examine the curricula, syllabi and to offer suggestions for the each Course Programme and to identify on whom the responsibilities for teaching will lie.

Chair : DoS.

Principal's Committee : each term / semester the Principal will bring together the whole management team, VP, DoS, Bursar, Programme Managers, and senior admin. staff. This meeting offers the opportunity for an update from the Principal down and for the other attendees to question and offer opinions about all aspects of the running of the college. *Chair : Principal.*

7] MONITORING AND INSPECTIONS

7.01 EDUCATIONAL

In order to offer bona-fide qualifications most colleges liase or enter into agreements with universities, other colleges or awarding bodies. Although a donor university is described in detail here, it can also be an agreement with another college or an awarding body.

The choice of which partner university is important and can be expensive; the higher level qualifications will cost the college more and cost the students more in fees than the lower qualifications; the more prestigious universities will charge higher fees than less prestigious ones.

The procedure is similar to this. The Principal or stakeholder suggests, or has contacts with, a university of suitable repute. The university is able to offer an appropriate qualification that can be

1] taught by and examined in the college (using material supplied by the university)

2] or taught in the college to a syllabus provided by the university but assessed by an externally set and marked examination.

There are other combinations of the elements provided and prescribed by the university, what is taught by the college and how the students are examined; sometimes course-work is accepted, with subjects set by the college and marked by the university or set by the university and marked by the college. All permutations are negotiated in advance and it is usually one or two years from inception before the first students start their course.

The university negotiates with the college on the following:

- The minimum admission standards for students
- The level of English ability required (see **appendix 9**)
- The fee to be paid by each student to the university (the per capita charge)
- The assessment procedure: who sets / marks exams / coursework etc
- Moderation: the requirement for another pair of eyes-appointed by the university- to look closely at work of high, average and low merit to ensure consistency
- Inspection: the university reserves the right to visit the college and observe all aspects of the course delivery
- The dates of examinations
- The dates of meetings to hear reports on the marks for coursework, exams etc and to agree 'Pass lists'
- Procedures for students who fail or do not attend for assessment
- Attitudes to plagiarism
- The qualifications and experience required by teachers delivering the course
- The facilities where teaching, learning and self-study are to take place

7.02 GOVERNMENTAL

In order to ensure certain minimum standards for colleges, especially those who recruit students from outside Great Britain, the government has established inspection procedures and inspection bodies. These bodies offer 'accreditation' or approval to the colleges. Students from outside the United Kingdom who wish to attend colleges which do not have accreditation, may have difficulty in obtaining visas to study in Great Britain.

7.02.01 THE BRITISH COUNCIL / BRITISH ACCREDITATION COUNCIL

It may often be thought desirable to spread knowledge of the college through the British Council and if it considered advantageous for the college to be publicised in all world-wide British Embassies and Consulates, the college must be 'recognised' by inspectors from the British Accreditation Council (BAC). This word 'recognised' means that the college has been inspected and has met various criteria and the facilities are recognised as being of acceptable standard.

These facilities include:

administration,
premises
academic resources
academic staff
academic management
teaching
welfare student facilities and its premises
financial stability

The British Accreditation Council [BAC] carries out inspections of colleges when requested (for which the college pays a large fee) and awards 'recognition' and a certificate to those colleges where the criteria set out above are acceptable. However, there may be areas where criteria are only minimally acceptable. If this is the case the BAC will re-inspect within a short period (for which another large fee is payable) to check for improvements. Once accepted and recognised, the certificate is issued (which can be used in college marketing) but more importantly, the college is listed on British Council websites and publications throughout the world.

These are the areas under which inspection takes place.

Management and Administration

The BAC will want to inspect:

Employers' Public Liability Insurance
Health and Safety Registration
Food Hygiene Registration (if there is a café)
Fire Safety Document
Payroll: evidence of payroll accounting system with evidence of deductions for PAYE (pay as you earn income tax) and NI (National Insurance)

VAT
CLA Licence (the licence to photocopy / scan from books and journals)
Staff Contracts
Staff Qualifications
Timetables
Student-learning Agreements and the distinction between compulsory and optional charges.
Staff Appraisal procedure
Marketing documentation
Procedure for dealing with poor or non-attendance

Premises

Classrooms: the inspectors look for a quality of accommodation identified in Section 2 above.

Facilities: these should include what is needed from the list in section 2.

Academic resources

The inspection looks at computer rooms, library facilities, and library content, material to stimulate the learners (posters, newspapers etc)

Academic Staff

By inspecting copies of the qualifications of the teaching staff, the inspectors evaluate how well qualified the staff are for the tasks they are employed to perform. It would be unusual for a teacher to have no professional qualifications at all and inspectors will penalise a college if this is the case.

Academic management

The structure of the senior management team, Principal, Vice-Principal, Director of Studies and Bursar is closely inspected. Syllabi are inspected, progression routes examined and procedures for examinations are discussed.

Teaching

All teachers available during the inspection will be observed. It is expected that teachers will provide copies of lesson plans and ancillary material to the inspectors.

Welfare - student facilities and premises

The inspection will involve not only the college premises but also the living accommodation of any students for which the college is in any way responsible. If the college offers 'home-stay' accommodation and places the students in board and lodgings, an inspection of some of these will be made. In addition, the procedure by which a student is allocated accommodation will be examined.

Financial stability

The examiners will wish to examine the accounts for previous years in order to discuss the financial stability of the college with the bursar and / or accountant. Procedures for collecting fees and for refunding deposits will be discussed.

An inspection of the college premises will be made where student facilities will be graded.

Questions will be asked about any leisure programmes offered or any sport facilities available; what is stated in the brochure or website must be delivered. Pastoral care - the treatment of students with problems- is also discussed.

Some weeks after the inspection, a report will be sent detailing the comments and observations in each of the principle categories; if all are satisfactory, the college will be recognised but if there are areas of concern, a recommendation will be made on how they are to be improved. After a further inspection, recognition can be made and the benefits of having British Council recognition can begin.

7.02.02 INVESTORS IN PEOPLE (IIP)

There are other organisations membership of which may have particular benefits for colleges; if it is intended to demonstrate the efficiency of the college's administration and concern for staff development, then the Investors in People (IiP) award may be one to acquire.

Again a series of inspections are involved and they focus on the way in which the staff manage and are managed and the way in which they interact with the students.

Focus is placed on clear and precise job descriptions with a consistent career structure in place. Contracts for both teaching and administrative staff are inspected and teaching will be observed under the same conditions as the British Council. The premises will be inspected but in most cases, the emphasis is on the staff and their well-being and how they function in their jobs.

The following are also UK government-organised bodies whose task is to ensure the high standards of educational colleges in Britain.

7.02.03 ASIC (Accreditation Service for International Colleges) is concerned with ensuring that 'vulnerable' foreign students are well looked after and well educated at colleges in UK. It also ensures that students are genuine and that their presence in UK is for educational purposes so ASIC works closely with the UK Border Agency. The intention is to ensure entry to genuine fee-paying students and prevent non-students entering the UK under the pretence of study.

The accreditation will initially assess the college's ability to meet the Home Office's minimum criteria for acceptance on a register of Education and Training Providers. Indeed, the recognition of ASIC as an accrediting body is based on its ability to reassure the Home Office that these criteria are being met.

In order to satisfy the needs of other stakeholders as mentioned above, ASIC has identified the following Areas of Operation, which will each be assessed and given a grade of Commendable, Satisfactory or

Unsatisfactory. These grades will not only be taken into account in deciding whether or not to award accreditation to a college, but will also be helpful in enabling students to make informed choices on where they might study.

Areas of Operation:

A. Premises and Health and Safety
B. Management and Staff Resources
C. Learning and Teaching; Course Delivery
D. Quality Assurance and Enhancement
E. Student Welfare
F. Qualifications and Awards
G. Marketing and Student Recruitment
H. Relationship with Government Offices and Reporting Mechanisms.

A College wishing to apply for accreditation under ASIC will need to demonstrate that it:

- Is a genuine education institution offering high quality academic or professional programmes, which are recognised by reputable bodies such as UK Universities, City & Guilds, Pitman's, EDEXCEL, ABE, OCR, ACCA etc. for articulation / advanced entry purposes to UK courses.
- Provides a suitable academic environment for students to enable them to be successful in their studies and to gain maximum benefit from their studies in the UK.
- Employs suitably qualified staff to teach and counsel students at the appropriate level.
- Provides a stable, safe and enjoyable atmosphere for study.
- Provides adequate support to students regarding welfare and study resources.
- Operates within the Home Office regulations regarding international students.
- Employs ethical marketing strategies in the recruitment of international students and has in place suitable monitoring processes to ensure compliance with Home Office regulations.
- Have suitable quality control procedures in place regarding the appointment and monitoring of education agents and representatives.

Their inspection procedures are similar to those of the British Accreditation Council and are not dissimilar to Ofsted.

The grades, which can be attributed by the inspectors to each of these areas are:

Commendable - representing good practice and a very good level of provision
Satisfactory - representing generally satisfactory practice and a level of provision, which meets the expected threshold standards for accreditation. Some minor shortcomings in provision may be acceptable, but the essential conditions specifically relating to immigration, have been met.
Unsatisfactory - representing weak/unsatisfactory practice with significant weaknesses, which do not meet the expected threshold standards.

7.02.04 OFSTED The Office for Standards in Education, Children's Services and Skills

This organisation has a remit to ensure that all providers of education, where funded by the state through grants, loans or awards to students, meets a minimum set of criteria. In the case of a college, funding is by way of loans to students studying in the post-compulsory sector for degrees, certificates, diplomas or professional awards.

Details can be found in the Handbook for inspecting colleges which is downloadable as a pdf file from www.ofsted.gov.uk

However, although the procedure is similar to that for British Council Inspections, it is more rigorous and, listed below are the major inspection items.

- complete and up-to-date data on enrolments and learners' achievements;
- course timetables (showing locations and staff);
- a self-assessment report (SAR) and any updated report;
- a college development plan, operating statements, curriculum plans, staff development plans and action plans arising from any previous inspections or course review or self-assessment;
- minutes from meetings of committees such as the senior management team, academic board, and equal opportunities committee;
- key policy documents, for example on assessment, key skills, staff development and lesson observation, together with the college charter;
- evidence of external links with schools and community organizations;
- evidence of the effectiveness of learner support activities, for example tutorial and additional support policies, with an indication of the numbers receiving additional support, careers advice and counseling;
- samples of learners' records and reports, including tutorial records and learning plans;
- course review reports or course self-assessment reports;
- details of the most significant resources, for example technological equipment;
- details of staff qualifications and experience and of staff development activity over the last two years; [see teacher training below]
- teachers' schemes of work, lesson planning and assessment records;
- samples of learners' assessed work;
- any other documents the college wishes to be considered.

OFSTED refers to a Self-assessment report (an SAR) and considers its inclusion as important because the SAR will provide inspectors with crucial evidence to evaluate the quality of leadership and management and the college's capacity to improve. In all inspections, the SAR will help the Lead Inspector to write the pre-inspection commentary. In inspections where areas of learning are examined it will inform the lead inspector's selection of which areas to inspect. During the visit, inspectors' findings will be compared with judgments in the SAR and discussed at team meetings and with the college.

Discussions with the principal, managers and teaching staff provide important evidence of roles and responsibilities, procedures and policies. They clarify how and why decisions are taken and how the impact of those decisions is evaluated. Inspectors may also meet, where possible, employers and sub-contracted providers, or partners jointly delivering, work-based learning, 14–19 learning, learn-direct, DWP, and adult and community education. Inspectors will also expect colleges to provide evidence of their links with employers and of arrangements to gather employers' views.

Interviews will be held with senior management and stakeholders. In particular, the role and responsibilities of the Principal and his guidance and leadership is examined. Leadership is about setting the direction of the college and establishing the culture. It is about doing the right things. Management is about systematically ensuring that day-to-day operations run smoothly and in the best interests of learners. It is about doing things right. Inspectors will distinguish between leadership and management. Where appropriate they may make judgments about the effectiveness of the principal as leader of the college. In their evaluation of leadership, inspectors will look at the degree to which the leaders:

- have a clear vision that is communicated to all staff
- have a relentless determination to improve learners' achievements
- inspire, motivate and influence staff and learners
- act as good role models for staff
- create effective teams
- are committed to running an inclusive college in which each individual matters
- produce development plans that reflect and promote the college's goals.

Finally, the report is compiled, discussed with stakeholders and senior management and presented under similar headings to those of the British Council:

administration,
premises
academic resources
Academic Staff
Academic management
Teaching
Welfare student facilities and its premises
financial stability

Grades on a four-point scale are awarded for each heading as below:

Grading scale

A four point grading scale will be used in all situations where grades denote summary judgments as well as where judgments are based on evidence such as lesson observations.

Grade 1 is outstanding,
Grade 2 is good,
Grade 3 is satisfactory
and Grade 4 is inadequate.

7.02.05 ENGLISH UK took over from ARELS The Association of Recognised English Language Schools during the last few years.

College membership of English UK offers assurances to students who are studying English as a Foreign Language that the teaching and facilities are of an acceptable standard and provide recourse should this not be the case. For colleges, where none of the students is less than 18, many of English UK conditions are less relevant; it is to be expected that students will be improving their language skills in order to undertake professional courses rather than learning English as a single subject. Nevertheless, membership of English UK can be advantageous to students when they select where to receive their college education.

English UK is now is the professional body of accredited, independent English language teaching establishments in Britain.

The Association represents over 400 member schools and colleges. They offer a broad range of high-quality general and specialist English language courses for adults and children at locations throughout Britain.

All members of English UK have passed rigorous inspections by the Accreditation unit of the British Council and are re-inspected every three years. Organisations with more than one course centre are inspected on the basis of a random selection of one in four centres inspected every three years.

English UK was formed in 2004 and has four main functions:

- To encourage members to raise their high standards even further;
- To represent the interests of members and their students to government ministers and other official bodies;
- To give students recourse to action if they have a complaint against a member school. If the Association cannot mediate between a school and student an independent Ombudsman is available to ensure fairness;
- To promote quality English language teaching in Britain both in the UK and overseas.

Quality Assurance

In addition to being accredited by the British Council, all member schools must abide by the English UK Code of Practice. This guarantees that:

- Teaching is of the highest standard; English UK has an extensive training programme to improve the already high standards of its members.
- Courses are designed to take account of age, country of origin and level of English.
- Schools seek and monitor feedback from students - this is used to improve and maintain standards.
- Schools and services must be described accurately in all advertising and publicity material.
- There are no hidden extra costs; English UK schools must give a clear statement, before registration, of all fees and charges for which students or their representatives may be liable.
- High standards of health and safety are maintained; schools must take all reasonable steps to protect students in their charge. Each school must have a student Welfare Officer and 24 hour emergency helpline.
- Accommodation is of a high standard; schools carefully check all student accommodation and ensure the suitability of host families if this accommodation is offered.
- Complaints must be taken seriously and resolved to the satisfaction of students. English UK has an established Complaints Procedure to which all members subscribe and an independent Ombudsman.

7.03 TEACHER TRAINING

Since 1992, it has been the intention of the Department for Education and Skills to train and to qualify all teachers in post-compulsory education. Apart from being desirable, it was the intention of DfES that it became compulsory. Ofsted inspectors will therefore examine to what degree the following are in evidence. In March 2009, the Government announced a shortened teacher-training programme where Qualified Teacher Status (QTS) would be offered in only 6 months. The current attitude to teacher training is:

new Initial Teacher Training (ITT) pathways and qualifications leading to the award of Qualified Teacher Learning and Skills (QTLS) status including specialist Skills for Life routes and Associate Teacher Learning and Skills (ATLS) status;

a requirement for all teachers, tutors, trainers and lecturers to fulfil at least 30 hours continuing professional development (CPD) each year, with reduced amounts for part timers;

a requirement for all teachers, trainers, tutors and lecturers to be registered with the Institute for Learning - www.ifl.ac.uk - a professional body;

a new leadership qualification (Principals' Qualifying Programme) for all new college principals;

Ofsted stated that:

all new teachers appointed from 1st September 2007 should have:

a 'Preparing to Teach in the Lifelong Learning Sector' (PTLLS) award, which is a minimum threshold licence to teach for all in a teaching role irrespective of job title;

a Diploma in Teaching in the Lifelong Learning Sector (or HEI equivalent - this can be a Certificate in Education [Cert.Ed.] or a Post-graduate Certificate in Education [PGCE]) at minimum level 5 leading to QTLS status for those in a full teaching role, including specialist Skills for Life routes;

a Certificate in Teaching in the Lifelong Learning Sector (or HEI equivalent) for those in an Associate teaching role, leading to ATLS status for those in teaching roles that carry significantly less than the full range of teaching responsibilities ordinarily carried out in a full teaching role and a period of professional formation, (the post-qualification process by which a teacher demonstrates through professional practice that they meet the standards, and can use effectively the skills and knowledge acquired in teacher training).

8] MARKETING

"Half of the money spent on advertising is wasted; the problem is we don't know which half'.
David Ogilvy (1960)

8.00 Marketing is the "engine" that drives industry. Therefore it is equally important for colleges as it is for Coca Cola; Heinz or Burger King. So, what is marketing ?

The best definition : *"it's the management process that identifies, anticipates and satisfies customer needs, profitably."*

In College terms it suggests : "providing good services for the student while making a profit ".

Businesses fail for 2 main reasons :

(1) Lack of finance

(2) Lack of marketing

The Marketing concept should be regarded as a philosophy. It makes customers (the students), and the satisfaction of their needs, the focal point of all business activities. It is driven by senior management, passionate about delighting their customers.

To ensure that marketing is successful you need to develop a marketing **plan**.

The basic components of the marketing plan are the marketing mix known as the 7 Ps – **Product, Price, Place, Promotion, and Physical evidence, People, Process.**

The concept is simple. Think about mixing ingredients for a cake. You need to get the right amount of eggs, flour and sugar. It is the same with the marketing mix; if the mix is wrong, the business will suffer.

8.01 The first P is **Product**, which is, for your purpose, the College.

This is the tangible, physical entity where the teaching takes place.

The quality of the product is important. For a College this can be identified by ASIC / BAC or other recognisable approval for example, which acts an external guarantor of certain quality standards.

Other attributes the Product, the College will need include: sufficient classroom space for the students; good, suitably qualified teaching / lecturing staff; adequate IT support; good toilet facilities for male and female students. These factors are described in chapter 2.

When assessing the quality of the Product / College, try to see it from the customer, the Student position and ask yourself the question "would you be happy studying here?

8.02 The second P is the **Price**. Price means profit for the college and value / quality for the student.

There are 3 possible strategies to use for Pricing the college services:

1) *Premium Pricing*: this is when a high price is used where a substantial competitive advantage such as when you have something special those other colleges do not have. An example would be London Business School who charge £30,000 for an MBA; their perceived quality is the reputation that their award is unique and World recognised.
2) *Penetration Pricing*: this is when a low price is charged in order to gain market share. Examples of this strategy can be found in London, East and West where there are many rival Business and Language colleges competing in the market In order to attract any students, the price must be low and more attractive than rivals.
3) *Economy Pricing* : where costs are kept at a minimum. An example would be a College that charges basic fees and pays teaching staff low rates.

Pricing is a key element for Colleges. Colleges fail by losing good lecturers through poor pay and the recruitment of cheap, non-qualified replacements. The students miss lessons and dissatisfaction spreads. Students leave : as we say, "they vote with their feet."

8.03 The third P is for **Place**.

For the purpose of colleges, place covers location, agents and the Internet.

Location: the college should be convenient for public transport so that it provides easy access for the students as explained in Chapter 1. To re-iterate, location should also be "fit for purpose "clearly identifiable as a college with reception areas, classrooms with whiteboards, tables and chairs; common rooms with food and beverage facilities. If the students have their own transport then parking spaces should be available.

Agents: these should be sole agents who represent your college only. In this role former students who know and like the College make excellent agents. Their only task is to recruit legitimate and motivated students to your college. Experience has shown that ex-students are usually more motivated and more results orientated. Motivation is very important and a college can provide this by backing up their agents with sufficient promotional material plus good commission rates (between 10% and 25 %). Set the Agents achievable targets and help them achieve them through appropriate support.

Internet: a good website can attract many potential students and it can be used in conjunction with agents; a student from Thailand who contacts the college can be put "in touch "with the local agent.

The Internet will also cover a wider global audience which most agents cannot reach. It is imperative therefore to establish a good IT system.

8.04 The fourth P is **Promotion.**

This involves all aspects of promoting (communicating) the college name to the World at large. It is important to use an integrated approach so that a single message is conveyed - often via. a logo, as explained in Chapter 1. Coca Cola for example uses its familiar red and white logos and retains themes of togetherness and enjoyment throughout its marketing communications.

Promotion is the most expensive part of the Marketing Mix and money has to be spent wisely. Coca Cola spends millions each year on promotion but as they made billions in profits it is money well spent.

These are some of the important aspects of Promotion / Communications for the College.

(1) AIDA (*Awareness, Interest, Desire, Action*). This is what customer / students need to get from your communication. They need to be aware of the college name and logo. They need to be interested in contacting you. After contact, they need to have both the desire and wish to join your College. The final stage is Action when the student sends the cheque for enrolment. If you can achieve AIDA in your communications this guarantees success.

(2) Personal Selling: this becomes a very important way to manage personal customer relationships. A personal visit by the Principal and senior college management to China, or any Country, will create trust and credibility because personal visits to various countries can result in 100s of students joining UK colleges. However, such personal visits can be very expensive and should be only used where there is the probability of a genuine return on investment.

(3) Sales Promotion [SP]: for Colleges the best types of SP are Diaries and Pens with College name embossed because this means the College name is on display 365 days per year. T-shirts and clothing with College name and Logo displayed by the students also promote the 'brand of the college.

(4) Public Relations [PR]. This is defined as the *"deliberate, planned and sustained effort to establish and maintain mutual understanding between an organisation and its public"*. Here, for a college, the public would include students / teachers / Local Authority, Stakeholders etc. It is relatively cheap and can make the college feel an important of the community. Press releases are part of PR and can be a very cost effective marketing tool *"Local College Head will be visiting Shanghai where he will be recruiting students for new business courses at our College in the High Road"*. Local papers are always interested in news relevant to the local community.

(5) Direct Mail: This is highly focused upon targeting consumers found upon an acquired database. Colleges could find databases, say, for Secondary schools in countries they were planning to visit and inform students of the future opportunities awaiting them at your College. Once you have been running a college for some years you can create your own database of past students as they may recommend their friends and relations.

(6) E Marketing: this is achieving marketing communication objectives by using the Internet. Think of the tools the Internet can offer to college marketing. Companies can *distribute* such as Amazon; companies can *build and maintain customer relations,* such as Dell; *money*

collection can be achieved online with Pay Pal. If the college has experts who have the IT skills plus marketing knowledge, e- Marketing can be highly cost effective and profitable.

(7) Trade Fairs and Exhibitions: A true statement gleaned from many years in the business is that the only people to make money at Fairs / Exhibitions are the Organisers !! Numerous British Council Educational Fairs are held on behalf of Universities but very few do any significant business. The more cost-effective approach is to organise your own bespoke event. Arrange this with your Agent and invite the people you and the agent want to see. At an organised 3 day bespoke fair in China on behalf of your college you will be able to interview students and arrange visas with British Embassy. The cost for a 3-day visit may be £2,000 but the income from the students selected may be over £150,000.

(8) Advertising: this is "paid for" communication. It is used to develop attitudes, create awareness (AIDA) and transmit information in order to gain a response from your target market. For colleges, the main advertising expense will be Brochure production. Potential students will want to see and to study a brochure. Therefore, it has to be a product that reflects the quality of the college. Other expenses may be advertisements in the Trade Press and local Press for students, teachers and staff. When planning advertising you need to consider the following:

- Who is the potential target audience?
- What do I wish to communicate with?
- Why is this Message important to them?
- What is the best medium for this Message - Newspaper or Poster etc?
- What would be the most appropriate timing?
- How much needs to be spent?
- How do we control our advertising?
- How is advertising success to be monitored?

8.05 The Fifth P is for **Physical Evidence**: This includes:

- The Building: is it fit for purpose?
- Internet / Web site: is it fit for purpose and easy to navigate?
- Brochures. Do they reflect the desired level of quality?
- Furnishings: seating, decoration; are they clean and appropriate and fit for purpose
- Signage and logos: well designed and widely displayed?
- Business cards. Well designed and do they reflect the desired level of quality?

8.06 The Sixth P is **People**: This is the most important element of any service, particularly in teaching. Whether the students are happy or not, will depend a great deal on the teaching. You need to ensure that

(1) Can the teachers actually teach as identified in Chapter 6? Just because the Teachers are qualified Accountants, or possess an MBA, does not mean they know how or are actually able to teach. They may have the knowledge but can they impart the knowledge to the students? It is recommended that all teachers have a teaching qualification.

(2) Can they empathise with the students i.e. can they facilitate?

(3) Are the students qualified to study the programme you are teaching i.e. always check their qualifications. In the classroom environment, it is sad to see students who are out of their depth. They can become demotivated and can equally demotivate the class. In a service industry, such as education, effective management and motivation of people (whether teachers or students) is a key element to the success of the business.

8.07 The Seventh and final, P is Process. This element looks at the ways the customer experiences the organisation's offering.

For a college the Process could work in the following ways:

(1) Speedy responses to the students' initial approach to the College.
(2) Advice and help given at all stages of the enrolment procedure.
(3) Prompt feedback to all questions.
(4) A 'meet and greet' service where students are met at the airport and taken to their accommodation.
(5) The availability of extra English classes /revision classes etc. for students who require them.
(6) Organisation of extra curricula activities for students such as visits to the theatre and historic locations.
(7) Provision of added value to all elements of the Process so that students are so happy with all aspects of the college that they recommend friends and family.

To sum up: marketing is all about adding and enhancing the customer/student experience.

If you can add value to the students' educational experience then the return on investment to the college will be considerable.

REFERENCES

BIBLIOGRAPHY

Bloom BS	1956	Taxonomy of Educational Objectives	London	Longman
Bruner J	(1960)	The Process of Education	Harvard UP	Boston
Bryden DA	(2007)	English for Business, Communication & Development	LSM Media	London
Bryden DA	(2003)	Fundamentals of Teaching in College and University	Athena Press	London
Buzan A	(2006)	Use Your Head	London	BBC
Childe D Holt +Rinehart	(1974)	Psychology and the Teacher	London	
De Leeuw E &M	(1990)	Read Better, Read Faster	Middlesex	Penguin
Goss, D	(1994).	Principles of Human Resource Management.		LSM
Hadfield J	(1997)	Classroom Dynamics	Oxford	OUP
Lozanov G	(1988)	Foreign Language Teacher's Suggestopedic Manual	New York	
Mace CA	(1969)	The Psychology of Study	Harmondsworth	Penguin
Maslow AH	(1943)	Motivation and Personality	New York	Harper
Mole J	(1995)	Mind Your Manners	London	Brealey
Pinker S	(1994)	The Language Instinct	Middlesex	Penguin
Robbins C	(1999)	The Test of Courage	London	Century
Skinner BF	(1953)	Science and Human Behavior	New York	Appleton
Solity J	(2008)	The Learning Revolution	Oxford	Hodder Education

Sprott WJH	(1958)	Human Groups	London	Pelican
Stenhouse L	(1976)	An Introduction to Curriculum	London	Heinmann
Stevick E And Hine	(1996)	Memory, Meaning and Method *a view of language teaching*	USA	
Underwood M	(1987)	Effective Class Management	London	Longman

APPENDICES

APPENDIX 1

PHRASES AND ACRONYMS

ALF	Average Level of Funding
ARELS	Association of Recognised English Language Schools
ASIC	Accreditation Service for International Colleges
B.Ed.	Bachelor of Education
BA	Bachelor of Arts
BAC	British Accreditation Council
BBCtv	British Broadcasting Corporation - Television
Cambs.	Cambridge University Examining Board
CELTA	Certificate in English Language Teaching to Adults
Cert.Ed.	Certificate in Education
C&G	City & Guilds of London
Dip.Ed.	Diploma in Education
DELTA	Diploma in English Language Teaching to Adults
DFES	Department for Education and Skills (superseded)
DIUS	Department for Innovation Universities and Skills
ECBE	European Council for Business Education
EEA	European Economic Area
FE	Further education (16+)
FEDA	Further Educational Development Association
FEFC	Further Education Funding Council

FENTO	Further Education National Training Organisation
fte	full-time equivalents
GCE	General Certificate of Education
GCSE	General Certificate of Secondary Education
GLH	Guided learning hours
HE	Higher Education
IiP	Investors in People
ITTC	International Teaching and Training Centre, Bournemouth
NLP	Neuro Linguistic Programming
NVC	Non-Verbal Communication (body language)
OCR	Oxford Cambridge and RSA Examinations Board
PGCE	Post-Graduate Certificate in Education
PITMANS	Pitman qualifications
QCDA	Qualifications and Curriculum Development Agency
TEFL	Teaching English as a Foreign Language
TEFLA	Teaching English as a Foreign Language to Adults
ToEFL	Test of English as a Foreign Language

APPENDIX 2

A] Bid Letter for Local Funding for Specific Course

B] Typical Bid document outlining the course for which funding is sought and the rationale of its need

A] Bid Letter for Local Funding for Specific Course

Name of college

Learning Skills Council – local area
Local address
For the attention of the Resourcing Manager

14 December 2010.

Dear Sirs,

Proposed Survival / Language Skills Course for the Somali Community

Our college works in the heart of the community in conjunction with other local colleges to provide education and training for undervalued and under-represented members of the local community.

Although we are currently engaged in providing courses for several minority groups, we have been unable to find franchise funding for a group of young Somali women who have only recently arrived in London and we are writing to you to bid for LSC funding to enable their re-education in English, numeracy and communication to begin in November. We have already :

- designed a syllabus and course programme *(copy enclosed)*
- prepared training material and put together a teaching team
- located premises
- fully costed the programme *(copy enclosed)*

We would be grateful if you would favourably consider this bid for funding as we feel that provision of such skills as we envisage will have continuing benefits for the Somali community in general and for the participants in particular.

Yours faithfully,

Principal

B] Typical Bid document outlining the course for which funding is sought and the rationale of its need:

Survival and Language Skills for Female members of the Somali Community new to London

Course Outline

Overview
A 15 week course for about 15 – 20 adult Somalis - mostly female - in the acquisition of English language, self-development and an introduction to living in London :

- Basic Numeracy, and how to buy things
- Verbal Communication, gesture and meaning
- Basic written English language, forms, signs and dates

Structure
The course provides for 180 GLH spread over 15 weeks (4 days / week x 3 hours / day) from February to June at 11 High Street, London

Assessment
The student Cohort will take OCN / Pitman Qualifications examinations in August.

Syllabus
1] Numeracy,

Calculations with and without calculators; decimal system; temperatures; quantities for buying produce; kilogrammes, litres and quantities for distance : yards and miles.

2] **Verbal Communication** pronunciation and enunciation; differences in defensible space; greetings, 'Where is...? 'What does it cost.' ' Can you tell me ...' Body language. , Job interviews

3] Basic English Language (reading and writing) roman alphabet**;** time, days, months, shopping lists reading signs and directions; letter formats for job applications; CVs; personal development.

Timetable

	Monday	Tuesday	Wednesday	Thursday
09. 00 -10.00h	Numeracy	Oral practice	Written English	'Life in London' (life skills practice)
10.00 - 10.45h	Oral practice	Written English (Reading)	Numeracy	Oral practice
10.45 - 11.05	Break	Break	Break	Break
11.05 - 12.00h	Written English (handwriting)	Life in London (life skills practice)	Oral practice	Written English

The above timetable will run for 15 weeks from February but near to the end of the course there will be guidance on portfolio preparation for the OCN examination or appropriate practice for the new ESOL core skills tests.

Resumé:

The 180 hour programme will equip the learners to be examined and obtain a formal and recognised qualification in English. However the course covers far more than just one qualification. Only 1.2% of Somali females attend college in Somali and the overall literacy rate is only 14%. Imparting the basic knowledge of oral and written communication with neighbours will liberate this vulnerable sector from many of the limitations illiteracy brings. Although the first award (and later Pitmans') qualification will be a valuable career recognition, the emphasis of the course will be on the development of self and communicative abilities - in accord with the new ESOL Core Curriculum – just as much as the award itself.

Management

The detailed programmes and lesson plans will be provided and managed by our college using a highly experienced and highly qualified team; we will arrange for selection of appropriate teachers, have them trained in appropriate methodologies, and draw up their contracts; the classes will be monitored for effectiveness and quality. We will purchase the necessary equipment and teaching realia needed for the course.

The local Somali Community Association have publicised the course within the community and demonstrated the suitability of those beginning the course. The minimum requirements for admission should include :

Motivation
A minimal knowledge of English language
Dedication
Ideas of a career path on conclusion of the course
Opportunities for continuing studies out of contact hours.

APPENDIX 3

ABRAM MASLOW'S HIERARCHY OF NEEDS DIAGRAM

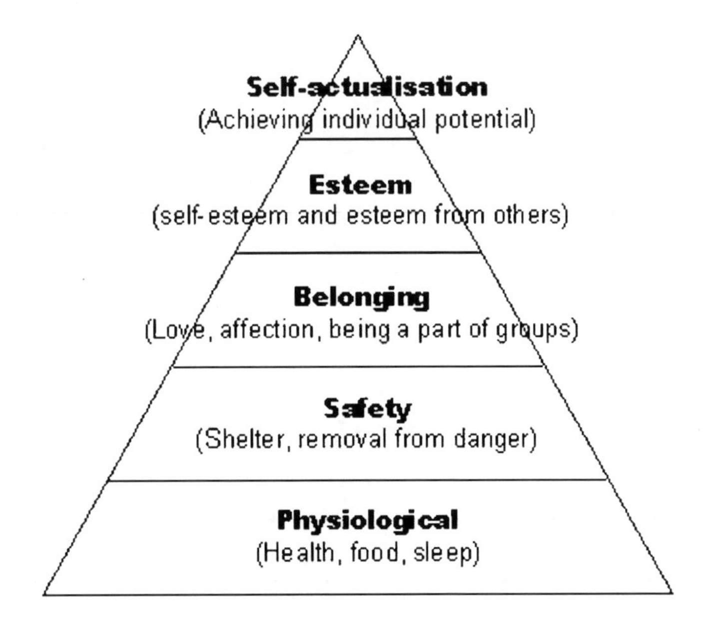

APPENDIX 4

SEATING DESIGN FOR LECTURE THEATRE

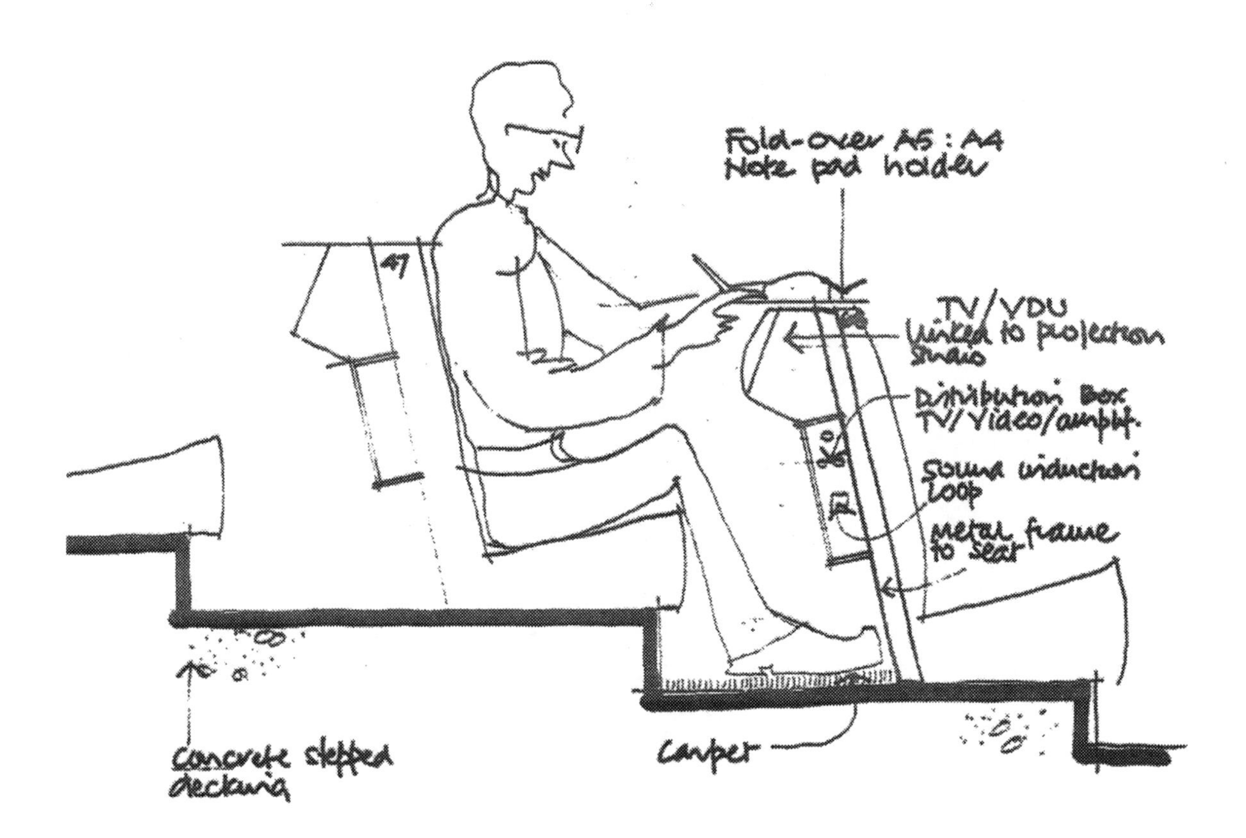

APPENDIX 5

THE DEWEY REFERENCING SYSTEM FOR BOOK LOCATION IN LIBRARIES.

The system is made up of ten main classes or categories, each divided into ten secondary classes or subcategories, each having ten subdivisions.

- 000 – Computer science, information, and general works
- 100 – Philosophy and psychology
- 200 – Religion
- 300 – Social sciences
- 400 – Languages
- 500 – Science and Mathematics
- 600 – Technology and applied science
- 700 – Arts and recreation
- 800 – Literature
- 900 – History and geography and biography

APPENDIX 6

TYPICAL ACADEMIC FOUNDATION / STUDY SKILLS PROGRAMME

week	RECEPTIVE SKILL	PRODUCTIVE SKILL [and grammar]	TUTORIAL HOUR	TEXT BOOK CHAPTER REFERENCES
1	Overview of programme: grammar : **parts of speech;** how we learn and forget; **summaries**; note taking; **mind maps. Communication theory**	Respond to 'how to learn' quiz; Identify nouns and verbs in text	produce mind map Write summary	**1, 6** **2**
2	Research methods; primary and secondary data; ***attribution*** + Harvard ***referencing;*** grammar : **reported speech Critical analysis**	Indirect speech Conditional tenses. Critical analysis: being able to examine processes, systems, objects, artefacts, issues and ideas in terms of their component parts and to make informed judgements about their worth, as well as the value and relevance of information therein.	Write references / correct book list errors	**7, 8,** **14**
3	Locale PAST PRESENT AND FUTURE. Form groups to plan collection of primary and secondary data for assignments	Organisation; planning; analysis Exercise : reported speech. Methods of data collection, questionnaires sampling etc. *Report format*	Test FORMATIVE (1)	**8,**
4	PRIMARY DATA COLLECTION	note-taking, observation, sampling and questionnaires	Analysis of data collection and research skills methodology	**8, 10**
5	Results of TEST (1) feedback Essay format	Paragraphing. Structuring essays incorporating attribution. *subject verb agreement; connectives*	Plan an essay; construct 3 paragraphs	**11**
6	Summary of requirements for report	Identify assignment to be written up as a report; *passives*; *adjectival order*	Test FORMATIVE (2)	**10**
7	Results of TEST (2) feedback	Reflective log	Prepare written analysis of 2 classes	**11**
8	Oral presentation [1]	Skills practice in making an oral presentation	Prepare group presentation	**4, 12**
9	**Oral presentation** [2]	Group presentations :	***oral presentation*** (assessed 20%)	**12**
10	Overview, , submission of ***Written Report*** and ***reflective log*** (assessed 80%)	SUBMISSION OF REPORT		

APPENDIX 7

Lesson Plan

Business Presentation Skills

Lesson 4 / 12

Aim : to identify written recruitments skills
Objectives : to write effective recruitment advertisements
To identify the components of job specification

Item	Stage	Interaction	Activity	Reason	Time
1	Warmer	S/s	Group discussion 'jobs I've done'	To think	7
				about	
		t	"look at today's programme …on board"…	employment	
	Brain-storm	T / ss	"what conditions / benefits would you look		
2			for when applying for a job?" (t monitors and		5
			elicits salary/ location/pension/ holidays /	Share	
			qualifications/	knowledge	
			prospects etc		
			t writes up responses		10
3	instruction		'now you are going to work in groups of 3"		5
	Develop-		prioritise conditions in groups x 3 and prepare		
4	Ment	Ss	reasons for group choice		
				Consensus	
	Challenge		"Read this" (show OHP of **handout 1**)		3
5	Question	T	"Would you apply for this job? Give reasons		5
6		T	"Write down 5 reasons why you would / would		
			not apply.	Analysis	5
	Comparison		Discuss with you partner		5
7		S/s			
				reinforcement	
	Exposure				5
			Ss offer reasons		
8	Comparison	Ss / t			
			Read this (distribute **handout 2**) and highlight		7
		T	the differences between the content of the 2		
			advertisements		
9					
	Feedback		Ss explain their own highlighted differences		10
		Ss / t	and one s compares by summary and t lists on		
			board; red for bad, blue for good		
10	stimulus	t	Before we break for coffee in 10 minutes,		
		ss	In your groups of 3 write down 5 questions		
			that are not answered by the advertisement in		10
11			handout 2		
			C O F F E E		

APPENDIX 8

EXAMPLES OF APPRAISAL FORMS

NAME:

ROLE:

DEPARTMENT:

APPRAISER'S NAME:

DATE COMPLETED:

DATE OF LAST APPRAISAL:

OBJECTIVES	ACHIEVEMENTS	NEXT STEP

PART 2 LOOKING BACK – REVIEW OF COMPETENCIES

COMPETENCIES	LEVEL ACHIEVED			COMMENTS BY WHEN
	Not OK	OK	Good	
COMMERCIAL AWARENESS				
TEAMWORK				
COMMUNICATION LANGUAGE SKILLS UNDERSTANDING				
KNOWLEDGE OF AVAILABLE COURSES				
SELLING AND INFLUENCING				
CREATIVE THINKING				
TIME-KEEPING				
MOTIVATION				
IT SKILLS				
TELEPHONE SKILLS				
VERBAL SKILLS				
CUSTOMER FOCUS				

LOOKING BACK – REVIEW OF LEARNING & DEVELOPMENT

LEARNING AND DEVELOPMENT OUTCOMES What skills, knowledge and abilities have you acquired since your last appraisal?	BENEFITS AND IMPACT How have these skills, knowledge and abilities made a difference to your work & achievement?

PLANNING FOR LEARNING & DEVELOPMENT

FOCUS FOR DEVELOPMENT What areas of knowledge, skill & ability do you need to learn or improve to help you do your job & achieve better results?	ACTION & REVIEW DATES What actions or steps should be taken to achieve this?

APPENDIX 9

ENGLISH LANGUAGE GRADE COMPARISON CHART

IELTS	Cambridge	ToEFL	ToEFL (on line)	TOEIC	Pitman	Council of Europe	Level	National Qualifications framework (UK)
9.0								
8.5	CPE	670+	293+	900	Advanced	Mastery	7	Level 5 (1st degree)
8.0								Level 4 NVQ 4
7.5				890				
7.0	CAE	600	250	810	Higher Intermediate	Effective Operational Proficiency	6	Level 3 [A level] NVQ 3
6.5*				730				Level 2 [GCSE a-c]
6.0		530	197	660	Intermediate	Vantage	5	EL3 /Level 1
5.5	FCE			590				
5.0				520				
4.5		460	140	450	Elementary	Waystage	3	EL2
4.0	PET			380				
3.5		400	97	310				
3.0				220				
2.5	KET				Basic	Breakthrough	2	ELI 1
2.0								
1.5								
1.0					Foundation			

APPENDIX 10

TEACHER MONITORING FORMS

Provider…………………………………………………………..
Venue……………………………………………………………..
Date………………………………Time………………………………
Course……………………………………………………………..
GLH……………..Lesson No…………..of……………

Teacher's name………………………………………………………

Lesson Plan Y / N   Syllabus and Course Programme Y / N   Register Y / N

Learners : No in class : @ start………………..finish………………..

No interviewed……….

Comments

SECTION ONE – ANALYSIS

1.00 Preparation details

1.01 Lesson Plan Yes / No
If **YES** complete 1-4 below

1) Clear Aims and Objectives? Sufficient number?

2) Are objectives suitable, appropriate, realistic, achievable?

3) Does the plan allow for : flexibility, checks on learning, variety?

4) Is the combination of content and method appropriate to ;

   a] the lesson's objectives?

   b] the learners' previous experience

2.00 Performance

2.01 Opening, recording attendance, voice, manners, questions, delivery, discussion, teacher talk V. learner talk. Variety in methodology; particular requirements; checks on learning; use of learners' prior knowledge; peer group learning; learning ownership.

Board work; appropriacy of course material; treatment of latecomers.

3.00 Evaluations

3.01 What visual aids / resources are intended to assist in the lesson?

3.02 Listening and observational skills of the teacher.

3.03 How appropriate was the pace and level of the lesson?

3.04 How was lesson progress related to learner response? Was it adjusted as required?

How?

3.05 What learning checks were used?

3.06 Other comments

4.00 Social relationships

4.01 Attitude of teacher to learners

4.02 Attitude of learners to teacher

4.03 Group dynamics and inter-action

5.00 Plan of class layout

6.00 Final assessment of teacher delivery

7.00 Assessment of learner progress

Teacher's comments

Teacher..Assessor........................

SECTION TWO –
RECOMMENDATION, CONCLUSION, FEEDBACK AND ACTION

1.1 Preparation

1.2 Performance

1.3 Social relationships

2.04 Management of materials and classroom environment

APPENDIX 11

COLLEGE INCOME AND EXPENDITURE ANALYSIS

The total INCOME, all the money taken in each year, sections A to E = **100%**

Expenditure on BUILDING COSTS section F, and SERVICING COSTS section J should equal approx. **35% of INCOME**

Expenditure on EMPLOYEE COSTS section G, SUBCONTRACTOR COSTS section H, PROFESSIONAL FEES section I, and SECTION K should equal approx. **35% OF INCOME**

SURPLUS / PROFIT FOR RE-INVESTMENT should equal approx. **30% OF INCOME**

LEGEND : **ss = students**
£ = cost in GBP
£p,£q = equals yearly cost of separate college courses
PAYE = Income tax deductions from salary
Non PAYE = free-lance teachers who are paid in full with no deductions

INCOME		£/year		NOTES
Fees from A	Private students Programme 1 x ss x £p Programme 2 y ss x £q Programme 3 z ss x £r etc			
	TOTAL A			
B	Government fees Programme 1 x ss x £a Programme 2 y ss x £b etc			
	TOTAL B			
C	Entrepreneurial income			Inc. food / drink concessions
	TOTAL C			
D	Fees from successful course bids			
	TOTAL D			
E	Interest			Balance of deposits earning interest
	TOTAL E			
	TOTAL INCOME			

EXPENDITURE				
	Rent / mortgage			Month x 12
	Local property taxes			Assume minor increase from previous year
	Utilities : gas, water, electricity, telephone			Assume minor increase from previous year
	Broadband / satellite TV subscription			Inc.VAT
	Repairs and renewals			Inc. accidental damage
	Insurances			3rd party, property etc
	TOTAL BUILDING COSTS			
	Administrative Salaries + NI			Inc.Principal.VP,DoS.Bursar
	Teaching staff salaries + NI			
	Other staff + NI (cleaner, handy man etc)			
	TOTAL EMPLOYEE COSTS			
H	Non PAYE teachers + holiday allowance on-costs			On-costs = approx. 11%
	Casual self-employed staff [agency]			Inc.VAT
	TOTAL SUB-CONTRACTOR COSTS			
I	Solicitors' fees			Inc.VAT
	Accountants' fees			Inc.VAT
	Agents' fees			Inc.VAT
	Marketing costs inc. advertising exhibitions, fairs etc			Excluding salaries Inc.VAT
	Bank charges			Negotiated
	University fees			% of ss fees passed on to partners
	TOTAL PROFESSIONAL FEES COSTS			
J	Printing charges – brochures / certificates			Inc.VAT
	Photocopier leasing			Inc.VAT
	Stationery costs			Inc.VAT
	Web design and maintenance			Inc.VAT
	Postage			
	Transport and travel			
	Membership subscriptions			To awarding bodies and professional bodies

	TOTAL SERVICING COSTS			
K	Depreciation			15% - 20% on value of capital equipment to be replaced
	Acquisitions : books, magazines			
	TOTAL EQUIPMENT COSTS			
	TOTAL INCOME			__ minus
	TOTAL EXPENDITURE			
		=		**SURPLUS/ PROFIT**

About the Author

A chartered surveyor, David began teaching on RICS courses in the late 1980s moving on to become Course Director for the Built Environment Degree Foundation year offered by South Bank University.

After obtaining a degree in Education, further teaching qualifications and a Dip. Ed. from the University of Sussex, David's interests became more specialised on the needs of learners who rather than studying in their native language, were studying in English. This led to a TEFL qualification from ITTC Bournemouth and to further research into teaching methodologies completed at London City College, Schiller International University and while working in Moscow, Shanghai, Siberia, Switzerland and France.

This was followed by work with DfES on Key Skills and basic level literacy and with City & Guilds on various teaching qualifications. For ten years David has been involved in teaching business subjects to students for whom English is a second language and for 6 years David has been running his own programme for new undergraduates and Masters' students titled *'Learning how to learn'* an academic foundation study skills programme identifying how higher grades can be achieved by more focused research and writing. He continues to develop teacher training programmes for several clients throughout the world.

His book 'Fundamentals of Teaching in College and University' is an acclaimed course book, used on many teaching programmes. His publication 'English for Business, Communication and Development' was published in 2007. His current activities include course design and curricula for programmes in the Middle East and China as well as roles in college management in London.

INDEX